PAIN *to* PURPOSE

My journey to redemption

Christina,

Wishing you all the best
on life's journey especially as we
learn to navigate this season that
is so unprescedented. I hope that
through my story you can be
ministered even if in a small way.
Family is crucial right now and
holding on to love ones and the
Lord is what's needed. All the
best.

Sidney

PAIN *to* PURPOSE

My journey to redemption

SIDONEY SAMUELS-BUCKRIDGE

This book is intended to provide informative and helpful information on the
subjects addressed in the publication. It is being made available with the
understanding that the author is not engaged in rendering health, medical,
mental health or any other kind of personal professional services in the book.
The reader should consult his or her health, medical, mental health or other
competent professional before adopting any of the suggestions in this book
or drawing conclusions from it.

Unless otherwise noted, Scripture   s are taken from the Holy Bible, King
James Version. Public Domain

Front Cover Photo by Vijay Britto

ISBN (paperback): 978-1-7361388-0-9
ISBN (ebook): 978-1-7361388-2-3

Library of Congress Cataloging-in-Publication Data

Name: Samuels-Buckridge, Sidoney, author.
Title: Pain to Purpose: my journey to redemption
Identifiers:
Library of Congress Control Number: 2020925788
ISBN: 978-1-7361388-0-9

Made in the United States of America

To the amazing women who have had the most impact on my life:

My hardworking and tenacious mom,
Pearl Tomlinson

and

My dear Godmom,
Kathryn Clark

Thank you both for believing in me... instilling values that have
served as my moral compass...and for inspiring me
to be the best version of myself—I would not be who I am today
without your wisdom, guidance and belief in my abilities.
I love you both.

TABLE *of* CONTENTS

INTRODUCTION

My name is Sidoney Samuels-Buckridge. I am a mother, wife, daughter, sister, an immigrant, and most importantly, I am a woman of faith with a passion to tell my story. My journey started in Kingston, Jamaica, and took me to the United States where I've lived my adult life. Why did I write this book? This book is my testimony and I wrote it in the hopes that I can help someone in pain. I sincerely believe that my journey will help someone who has dreams, visions, and aspirations that are not coming to fruition. You might have encountered a situation that knocked the wind out of you, and you asked, "What now?" I hope you can learn how I pulled myself up when the walls came crashing down. My perspective may be different from yours because of my immigrant background and the way I view the American culture, but the lessons I learned along the way transcend age, gender, race, and culture.

My faith continues to be a stronghold in my life. I learned along the way that I would not have made it without the Lord Jesus by my side. My faith in God gave me hope even when it seemed I had nothing to be hopeful for. He is such a forgiving God who never gave up on me, just like a parent will never give up on a child. While I have been journaling my entire life, surprisingly, I had never gone back and read what I wrote in my journals until I started to write this book. What I found written down in black and white startled me. It was eye-opening and emotional to look at my 20-year-old self through the lens of a 45-year-old. I found myself struggling as I relived some of the most painful aspects of my life.

What you will get from this book is a transparent account of one immigrant's plight to experience the "American Dream" that everyone talks about. I made mistakes and learned lessons, and with God's help, I was able to find love and contentment. This book is a labor of love, for I've always wanted to be a writer. For as long as I can remember, I've always had a pen and paper, scribbling down stories for the book that I would write one day. That one day and the inspiration that finally motivated me to start writing my book occurred when I unexpectedly attended an Impact Junkie workshop for entrepreneurs at my church. I went there for one purpose and left having discovered another—the outline for this book. The organizers impressed upon the attendees to pursue something that brings passion. As I sat there scribbling in my notebook, this memoir took form. I was so excited as I drove home and said, "Lord, this is the clarity that I needed."

The timing of my writing was also no accident. As the world around me changed due to the pandemic associated with COVID-19, writing this book provided a creative outlet and helped me to deal with some of the dark forces of my past. I was also able to celebrate how far I have come on this journey of life. There were times when I cried as I relived some of the hurts from my past, but there were also times when I rejoiced over major accomplishments. Along with everyone else, I remained sheltered in place for months on end, confronted with dismal news from around the world. My children stayed home learning virtually while I was working remotely and managing work and home. Writing in the evenings and weekends helped me relax and gave me a much-needed distraction.

When I was going through my trials, I wished I could have learned from someone else in a similar situation. I will keep it real with you. When you read this book, you will discover that I share the high and low points in my life. Sharing such intimate aspects of my life with the world was something I debated with myself, but I went with transparency. I lay it all out here to bring encouragement to others, and I hope someone can learn from my mistakes and apply the knowledge from situations where I behaved correctly. This book is for someone in pain, whatever the source of the pain might be.

I have been journaling most of my life, and I continued this practice throughout my life: during the pinnacles of success and the valleys of agonizing defeat. Journaling helped me get in tune with how I was feeling. There were times when I wanted to scream out my frustrations, but instead, I silently wrote those thoughts in my journal. Throughout the book, I share excerpts from my journals as well as from letters that I sent to my family during my early years in the United States, when letter writing was still a preferred means of communicating with friends and loved ones.

I'm also hoping that my fellow immigrants will be able to relate and reflect upon their own similar or different paths. This book is for everyone who is interested in learning how to navigate life in order to accomplish their dreams—whatever those dreams are.

Sidoney

Chapter 1

WHEN OPPORTUNITY COMES KNOCKING

"In the middle of difficulty lies opportunity."

—Albert Einstein

Today, I am a successful Jamaican immigrant living in the United States, with a promising career and a beautiful family. It hasn't been an easy road though. As a child, I had a humble beginning. But with a great support system and an inner drive to overcome obstacles, I've been able to succeed in my personal and professional life. As a dark-skinned Black woman, I've had to learn how to navigate these obvious realities in order to get what I want. As I share from my life, I also realize some of the tradeoffs I've had to make along the way.

I come from a family who didn't have much materially, and my parents struggled to provide the basic necessities. By the age of 18, my mother, Pearl, had two babies a year apart on her hands. My biological father, Lloyd, a philanderer, was nowhere in sight. His hazel eyes and light complexion meant that he was popular with the ladies, and he had no plans of settling down to domestic life.

To say my mother struggled is an understatement. She was in the capital of Jamaica with no family around, little support, and two small babies relying on her for their every need. Some would say that I was lucky to be alive in 1974 when I came into the world as a preemie at six months and two weeks, weighing only two pounds. In fact, for two whole weeks from the time I was born, my mom never saw me because I was in an incubator. She feared the worse—her baby had died, and the nurses were lying to her. After pleading with the nurses, she was allowed to see me.

My older brother Carey was born deaf and suffered from a mild case of mental retardation. It is difficult enough for a teenage mom to manage on her own, much more with a child with special needs. When I was five years old, my dad was murdered during a very violent and turbulent time in Jamaica due to political unrest. I had the misfortune of seeing my dad lying on the ground in an abandoned building the morning his body was discovered. There was blood everywhere. That was my first time seeing a dead body, and I froze for what seemed like forever, even as I listened to the conversations of the adults around me. At that time, I didn't understand the permanence of what happened—I wouldn't see him again? How could that be? The day before, Carey and I spent the whole day with my dad. We'd gotten on his back, and he tickled me so hard that I had tears in my eyes. My dad wasn't a staple in my life, and my brother and I saw him only occasionally, so I treasure my last memory of us having him for a whole day. During that time, it was our stepfather, George, who was the constant father figure in our lives.

With my mom's seventh-grade education and her husband's less than that, employment opportunities were limited. We lived in a not-so-nice neighborhood. There were times when our meals consisted of nothing but carbs and vegetables, and meat became a treat for Sunday dinners. But I remember when I was six years old and in grade one at Halfway Tree Primary School, my Mom would dress me nicely in my school uniform and send me off to school. There was usually no money for me to buy lunch at school; however, my stepdad would sometimes come to my school to give me money for lunch from what he received as a day laborer. Needless to say, that made me feel fortunate.

Early in life, I lost myself in books. I was an avid reader who couldn't get my hands on enough. When other girls my age wanted dolls for Christmas, I wanted books. I would frequently find myself curled up on the verandah reading, whisked away to places I could only imagine in my mind. My favorite books were fiction, but over the years, my desire to read other genres broadened exponentially. Ultimately, my passion for reading cultivated the woman I am today.

As a little girl, I found myself praying to God, most times when I wanted material things. I prayed for a beautiful dress to wear to church, I prayed when I wanted money to buy a book, and I prayed when I wanted meat with my dinner. I didn't know, however, that this was the beginning of a faith that would develop and see me through some rocky places in my life.

Growing up poor in Jamaica had other challenges too. Jamaica had a strong "class system." It was difficult to move out of the class that you were born into. Even at a young age, as I looked around my neighborhood, I knew that I wanted something better for myself. After all, I wanted to be like those girls I read about in books. They had lovely clothes to wear, amazing families, and choices. What I read about in my novels was far from the reality I saw around me. As soon as girls became teenagers, they sought refuge in the arms of a man. Many times, these men had little to offer them. It was easy to tell these young ladies not to go down that road. However, that was all they saw around them. Many parents were barely surviving themselves, and these young ladies had to fend for themselves. What they got from the men was money, clothing, or sometimes their only means of survival.

Despite our circumstances, one thing I was blessed to have was a mother who was determined that I would have a better life than she did. She worked hard to provide for our basic needs. What else stopped me from following my peers? I got involved in the church at an early age, and that became my lifeline.

When I was eight years old, I started attending church. It's interesting that my mom was not a Christian then but she got me dressed every Sunday morning and we both took the five-minute walk so that she could drop me off at Sunday school at Open Bible Church, and one of the teachers would walk me home afterward.

I was like a sponge and soaked up all the knowledge that I learned. Soon, Sundays alone were not enough for me and I became active in church. I started attending the prayer meeting during the week. I also attended Vacation Bible School and participated in the Easter programs and in Visionette— a program designed to educate and groom young Christian girls. Church became my second home. When I turned nine years old, I was baptized and I gave my life to the Lord. At that age, I'm not sure I fully understood what I was doing, but I enjoyed the teachings and the company of the people I was interacting with at the church.

Many of the women took me under their wings to ensure that I was living my life in a Christ-like manner. In retrospect, they were concerned that I did not have a Christian role model at home, so they wanted to make sure that I had help in my walk with God. Even when I was undeserving, God never left me.

He was always there at the opportune time through my various stages and seasons.

When I was 10 years old, in grade six in primary school, Mom got a cleaning job from an American couple, Kathryn and Jay. Looking back at that time, I had no idea how pivotal this relationship would be to change the trajectory of my life. Sometimes Mom would take me with her when she went to work. She always warned me to be quiet and to not touch anything. While she cleaned, what did I do? I would first do my homework and then lose myself in one of my books. I didn't mind going with my mom at all because it was quiet and Carey and my one-year-old brother Dwayne were not around to distract me.

When I started going with my mom, the first thing I noticed was just how tall her employer was. To a 10-year-old, Jay seemed like a giant at well over six feet tall. At first, I was a bit scared, but you can always tell how a person is by the things they do. I was always impressed by how he would pick mangoes for my mom. His acts of kindness were not lost on this little girl. His wife Kathryn always stopped to ask me what I was reading. Of course, I would light up and share every single detail that I could remember.

Kathryn took an interest in me and would frequently inquire about how I was doing in school. She would ask my mom about my grades and how I was getting along. I was a decent student, and Mom would share my report cards. Kathryn traveled all over the world because of her job. She worked for Special Olympics International and headed up the organization's Caribbean office. I really loved when she traveled because she would bring back a new book or two for me. That was always such a treat. Going to the library was my favorite pastime, but these books she gave me did not have to go back. They were all mine. And that made such a huge difference to a 10-year-old.

In grade six, I took the Common Entrance Exam, which was the standardized test that determined which high school a student would attend. Although the odds were stacked against me, I was determined to get into one of the top-tier schools. While other children were watching television or playing, I was studying. I studied very hard because I knew that if I got an opportunity to attend one of these schools with the best teachers, superb facilities, and with other students who were the best of the best, I was convinced that I would be on my way to achieving success. Talk about pressure, this one exam carried so much weight for a child so young. When I was exhausted... I studied. When I had free time...I studied. After finishing my homework...I studied. When I got home from church... I studied. When others gave up...I studied.

There was a debacle the year that I sat the exam. Allegedly, there was a cheating scandal at many schools across the island. My school, Half Way Tree Primary, was identified as one of the schools that cheated. I had no idea what all that was about. I remember sitting in the classroom on the day of the exam, praying to the Lord to help me through the test. But because of that allegation, all the students at my school were required to retake the exam. I sat in a room yet another time, praying to God to help me do my best so that I could pass the exam.

The results of the exam were printed in the local newspapers, from which students could find out which high school they qualified to attend based on their exam scores. To my dismay, my name was not there. We immediately knew that something was wrong. I knew the exam wasn't more difficult than normal and I studied really hard for it. I was so disappointed. I felt broken and I cried. Mom went into action mode and reached out to a family member to see if she could get me into a high school. There were some top-of-the-line high schools that everyone dreamed of attending. At the top of my list were

Campion College, Holy Childhood High School, and Immaculate High School. To be accepted at one of these top-tier schools, you needed an exceptional score on the Common Entrance Exam. While I was glad that my mom was able to get me into a high school, it was not one of my choice schools. And while everyone was happy that I was going to a high school and not a secondary school (those who didn't get the top grades went to secondary schools), I was not happy because I put in a lot of work and I couldn't understand what happened.

A few days later, Mom received a telephone call from the principal of my school to explain that there was a problem at the newspaper and they mistakenly did not print the names of students who passed the exam with surnames from S to Z. Mom was instructed to go to the Ministry of Education to receive my school assignment and the notification to take to the school that I passed for. When she went to the Ministry of Education, they informed her that I passed for Campion College, which was my first choice. Unfortunately, due to the mix-up, my first choice that I passed for was now full and they found me a spot at my second choice, Holy Childhood High School. To say I was overjoyed when I received the news would be an understatement. To know that the Lord had my future in his hands and He answered my prayers further strengthened my faith.

Back then in Jamaica, high school placement was your ticket to start your school career on the right footing. The top-tier high schools had the most resources, better-skilled educators, and more opportunities for learning and development. Unlike the United States, during that time not everyone went to high school and high schools were not all created equally. In addition, the class system in Jamaica played a role in these school placements as well. No one will ever say this, but we all knew that children from my neighborhood had limited opportunities to get into the top-tier schools. Looking around the neighborhood, every year you would see only a handful of students passing the exam for these sought-after high schools.

My hard work paid off. Sidoney Sasha Samuels from the ghettos of August Town in Kingston passed the Common Entrance Exam and was accepted to Holy Childhood High School! My family was ecstatic. I was going to be the first in my immediate family to go to high school, not to mention one of the top-tier high schools in the country. My young mind could not really grasp what all this meant for my family. I knew Mom was proud because she told the news to everyone who cared to listen. During this early stage in my academic career, I was fortunate to have two mentors, before I even knew what that word meant. Andy and David were teachers living in my neighborhood who saw something in me and invested years in my development. They taught, coached, and guided me towards academic success.

Attending Holy Childhood, a Catholic all-girls high school, provided me with an education and opened my eyes to the societal norms that existed in Jamaica. The Jamaican school system follows the British system; therefore, high school is from grades seven through eleven. As a child, my faith was an integral part of who I was. Thankfully, it kept me grounded during my teenage years. I'm glad that I had that to keep me on the straight and narrow. I was very naïve when I entered high school. I learned a lot about myself and my faith, and being exposed to classmates from various socioeconomic backgrounds was eye-opening. A large percentage of my peers were from the upper class, and their realities were unlike my own.

It surprised me how much my peers took for granted. I listened to their complaints and I always wondered to myself what there was to complain about. They took trips to the United States for vacations, they had everything that money could buy, and they had all the latest and greatest material assets. Since I had so little, I was very grateful for everything I had. As I listened to them, I dreamed of a time when I, too, could experience these things—minus the complaints.

Peer pressure became real during my teenage years. I was tempted to explore things that my friends were experimenting with, but my faith and many conversations with my mom were always at the forefront of my mind. When I was nine years old, I had the "birds and the bees" talk with her. I'm not sure how it happened in other households, but in mine, Mom was definitely clear. She told me that there were two roads in front of me and I needed to choose one. I could stay in her house and she would work hard to provide for my needs and my job was to go to school and get an education. The alternative would be to make the decision to get involved in "grown folks" business, and if I made that choice and got pregnant, then I would be on my own. Basically, she said, "Keep your legs crossed." Even though I was young, I never forgot that talk and I made up my mind that I was going to choose the path of getting an education. It's easy to make that choice at nine years old, but things became challenging as a 13-year-old who wanted to fit in with her friends. However, my drive to change my circumstances and being surrounded by women of faith and other teens living for God kept me from succumbing to negative peer pressures.

When I was 13 years old, life became unbearable at home. My mom and stepdad were not getting along, and it affected me. I witnessed physical and verbal abuse. It was difficult to watch my mom go through that experience. I vowed to myself that I would never allow a man to disrespect me the way my stepdad did my mom. I always wondered why my mom stayed. She was a strong Black woman who made many sacrifices for her children. However, when it came to herself, I never understood why she didn't fight for something better.

Circumstances can dictate why a woman would remain in an unhealthy situation. While my stepdad was not the best husband, he was a provider, and Mom needed the financial help. As a domestic worker, she was not making enough to take care of three children. I was in high school and I needed school fees, expensive books, uniforms, and lunch money. Not only did Mom have me and my brothers Carey and Dwayne, but she was also guardian for my cousin Paula who lived with my family. She had four children to support financially.

At the time, I did not understand; I just wanted all the yelling and fighting to stop. My environment began to take a toll on me. My relationship with Kathryn had continued to develop over a three-year span, and she took a deeper interest in me. Kathryn became like a second mom to me, and I began calling her Godmom. Little did I know that she would become my fairy godmother! She perceptively noticed that something was wrong. I became withdrawn, and my grades began to slip. At first, when she asked me what was wrong, I was hesitant to open up. Things continued to deteriorate, and I did not want to be in that house anymore. I finally shared with her what was happening at home. I asked if I could come and live with her, stressing that I wouldn't be any problem. She explained to me that I couldn't live with her because of her work travel schedule and no one would be around to take care of me. However, she told me not to worry as she would work something out.

I felt hopeless. I feared that this would continue to be my reality, so I prayed hard to God to work it out. I remember sitting in church many Sundays, asking God to get me out of my stressful situation. True to her word, Godmom made a way when I thought there was none. God answered my prayers.

At Holy Childhood High, there was a boarding school on campus. A lot of the boarders were students who lived outside of

Kingston, the capital of Jamaica. Many of the boarders lived on the north and south coasts of Jamaica, in places like Ocho Rios, Negril, and Montego Bay. Boarding school mostly consisted of residents whose parents were well-to-do. Many of these parents were business owners, politicians, and those at the top echelons on the island. Godmom paid for me to go to boarding school, and I spent three years there. I was so glad to get away from my home life, but I experienced some challenges I could not have predicted. This experience taught me a lot about the country of my birth.

I had a mixed experience at boarding school. For three years, I lived there during the week and went home on the weekends. Living together with a group of other girl boarders taught us to rely on each other. A small part of me felt like I belonged when I was at boarding school. We ate dinner together, did homework together, and stayed up at night, giggling and sharing our dreams and aspirations. Unfortunately, the not-so-pleasant part of my boarding school experience occurred during my first year there. I was a boarder on the main campus, which is right where my school was located. It wasn't a secret that I did not have the financial means as the other boarders. I did not have fancy clothes, and I had an American couple, not my parents, paying my fees. The nuns who ran the boarding school treated me differently from the other children. I often wondered why, but living in this environment was one hundred percent better than what I experienced at home, so I didn't complain and just made the most of the challenges.

Why did the nuns treat me differently? I had numerous experiences pointing to the fact that they did not think I belonged at that boarding school with the children of the elites on the island. I would get in trouble with the nuns for the simplest of infractions. I remember one time I had a big test and stayed up in the bathroom studying for it because I wanted to do well.

The den mother (the woman who handled logistics) was doing rounds, and when she saw the light on in the bathroom, she talked to me about it and sent me to bed. However, when she reported it to the nuns, I was immediately disciplined.

This experience stood out in my mind because many of my fellow boarders did the same thing, and I never saw one of them punished for that. I was a reserved child who preferred to read than socialize with fellow boarders, but for some reason, this very reserved 13-year-old kept getting in trouble for things that just did not make sense. This was a new phenomenon for me because I was the type of child who never got into trouble. I shared what was happening at boarding school with Godmom. Needless to say, she was not happy about it; after all, she was paying the same money as the others. Still, the nuns treated me differently because I was from the lower class and they did not believe I belonged there.

Before that time, I lived around people who were in the same socioeconomic status as I, so I did not notice any differences. But I was determined I was not going to be deterred, and a little inconvenience was not going to set me back. I was resilient, and my solution was to push and work even harder. I poured myself into my schoolwork. I took the mistreatment in stride and I counted my blessings. I was now in an environment conducive to learning, where I was exposed to people living lives I only read about in books, and I was thriving.

God answered another prayer for me. Somehow, He was always there beside me. During my second year at boarding school, I was moved to another boarding facility off-campus and had a much better experience. Although both locations had nuns, most were at the first boarding school. Based on my experience, I thought most nuns were mean until I met Sister Elizabeth. I will never forget her because she treated me as a person of worth. She did not look at me like a kid from the wrong side of the tracks. Sister Elizabeth was the nun in charge of the boarding facility where I spent my last two years, and I had a good experience. I would share my dreams of what I wanted to do in life with Sister Elizabeth, and she never made fun of me or told me that my dreams were unattainable. She always encouraged me to do well in school and to work hard. Sometimes small acts of kindness can have a profound impact on a young person's life. That's what Sister Elizabeth did for me. She looked beyond my circumstances, and I will never forget her kindness.

During my last year of high school, Godmom and I discussed what my options were after graduation. We decided I would go to the United States to attend post-secondary school. We explored the possibility of going to a U.S. college, but given my age and the fact that my entire school career was under the British school system, she thought it best for me to attend grade 12 in the U.S. since high school in Jamaica stopped at grade 11. That would give me an introduction to the U.S. school system and make it easier to explore the possibility of college. At 16 years old, I graduated from Holy Childhood High School and was excited about the prospect of migrating to the U.S. At first, I was not thrilled to go back to high school because I had already graduated, but doing so provided an opportunity to leave the life that I knew and explore a whole other world and way of life. Getting to the U.S. was not an easy journey, however.

My First Experience with Racism

Jamaica's motto "Out of Many, One People" is very fitting because of the diverse cultures that reside on the island. Jamaica's population consists of Blacks, Chinese, Indians, Whites, and many bi-racial individuals due to the mixing of the various groups. While a class system exists in Jamaica, the issue of race has never been much of a problem. I had my first experience with racism at the U.S. Embassy in Jamaica's capital, Kingston. I was beyond excited to go to a foreign country. Everything was in place: I would attend J.P. McCaskey High School in Lancaster, Pennsylvania; I had picked my classes for my senior year; and Godmom had arranged for me to live with family friends who had kids close to my age. I had gotten my first Jamaican passport, and the last step was to go to the U.S. Embassy for an interview.

Godmom explained the process to me, but I was too excited to pay much attention to all the details. I was just interested in what my life would be like in another country. I remember the day like it was yesterday. It's funny how until that time, I'd never really paid much attention to Godmom being Caucasian. I went to boarding school with many different races of people—Chinese, Indians, Blacks, and Caucasians—so to me, it didn't matter. However, I quickly learned that for some Americans, race is a big issue.

At my interview, I thought the immigration officer was an exceptionally beautiful woman; she had long blonde hair and piercing blue eyes. At first, she asked Godmom some basic questions, which she promptly answered. Quickly, things took a turn for the worst as she began asking questions that did not sit well with Godmom. The comment that stood out the most was when the immigration officer looked at her and said, "Why should I give you a visa for this child? For all I know, you could be taking this child to the U.S. to become a servant." She handed back our paperwork, and she denied my student visa to go to the U.S. In the six years that I had known Godmom, I had never seen her cry. She cried throughout the whole taxi ride back to her house. She was very emotional and kept saying, "I would never do something like that." When we got back to her house, she was inconsolable. I didn't know what to do, seeing how emotional she was. What happened here? What did I do? What should I do? I remained quiet and went into my comfort zone; I grabbed one of my novels, and I curled up in a corner and started reading a book. While I wasn't emotional, I was saddened that my dream of going to the U.S. would be no more. At that time, however, I just didn't know how to deal with my emotions, and it was safer to lose myself in a book.

Basically, this immigration officer just saw a Caucasian woman and a Black female teenager. Forget the paperwork from the school showing I was enrolled; forget the letter from the host family that I would be living with, explaining that they were opening their home to me. All she saw was a Black teenager, and I couldn't possibly be anything other than someone's help. Forget that I had just graduated from one of the top high schools in Jamaica. None of that mattered. Godmom shared the experience with fellow Americans on her staff. She got on the phone and spoke to several of her contacts in the U.S. to explain the outcome.

J.P. McCaskey High School
P.O. Box 150
Lancaster, PA 17602
5 July 1992

To Whom It May Concern,

I am having trouble understanding why the application of Sidoney Samuels for a student visa has been denied. I have been involved with exchange students at McCaskey H.S. in Lancaster, PA. since 1965 and during that time have never known of a student who did not go home at the end of the school year or who was used as a house servant during the year.

Over the past 10 years, we have averaged eight exchange students per year at McCaskey—both program and private exchanges. Since John Syphard has been the principal of the school all that time, he has signed I-20 forms and is quite aware of what he is signing and why. Perhaps the person who denied Sidoney's application knows something about Mr. Syphard and is questioning his integrity.

Also, McCaskey High School has over 54% "minority" enrollment. The Black students in the school were thrilled to learn that we were going to have a Black exchange student this year. I have already received several phone calls from Black students wanting to know why the State Department had no problems approving the passports for the eight white exchange students we will be hosting this year but denied the only Black student. I have no answer for this and said only that I hope the decision was not racially motivated. The students are demanding a better answer than that and at this point I cannot give it to them.

I am hoping the person who made this decision will reconsider her action and Sidoney will be allowed to spend the coming year at McCaskey and live with the Lyall family. If this is not possible, I certainly hope Ambassador Holden will find the reason for the denial and inform Mr. Syphard or myself so that we can pass the information to the McCaskey students and the rest of the Lancaster community.

Sincerely,
George A. Resh
AFS Club Advisor

Lucky for me, Godmom was also a fighter who refused to give up. I felt so blessed that someone was fighting hard for my future. She reached out to her network, and we had multiple letters from congressmen, the head of the Special Olympics, the school I was to attend, and numerous people who vouched for her credibility. We obtained another appointment to the U.S. Embassy., Godmom was too traumatized by the rejection, so she sent me with Anna, one of her staff. The second time did it—I got the student visa, and I was on my way to the United States of America!

USA, Here I Come

In August 1992, I left the security of my family to embark on a new life. This was my first time getting on a plane. Godmom was right there beside me, holding my hand and guiding me every step of the way. Saying goodbye to my mom was one of the hardest things I had to do. Unfortunately, she did not have a visa, so she could not come to the United States. I was excited and nervous all at the same time. The questions that ran through my head were the norm: *Will I fit in? What if things go wrong? Mom and Godmom will not be there. How will I adapt to a new culture and new way of life?* Oh, I had butterflies in my stomach.

Godmom and I flew into Washington, D.C. That's where my journey in the United States started. I had my first stay in a hotel. I was now experiencing all the things I read about and saw on television, eating fancy foods that I couldn't even pronounce. I was like a kid in a candy store. I wanted to try everything. During my early days in the U.S., I was exposed to different types of food. Dishes like sloppy joes, lasagna, peanut-butter-and-jelly sandwiches, and waffles were nothing like my familiar Caribbean food. I immediately noticed that the spices that we used were visibly absent from the meals I was now eating, and that took some getting used to. Thank God I had Godmom with me. I could ask all the dumb questions and get them out of the way, so once I met the new family, I could be somewhat "normal."

Our next stop was Lancaster, Pennsylvania, which would be my new home. I had my own welcome party at the airport. I was so pleased that everyone was looking forward to my being here. It was overwhelming in a good way. I was introduced to my host family, Joe and Sally. They had teenagers close to my age and a beautiful home in the suburbs of Lancaster. I couldn't believe I would be living in a home like this—beautifully designed interior, great landscape both in the front and backyard—which I only saw on television.

I must thank Jim, Bev, Joe and Sally, family friends of Godmom, for the impact they had on my early American experience. They opened their home to a perfect stranger from a country and culture different from their own. My initial American experience was largely due to their guidance. The experience that stuck out most in my mind during my early days in the country was my "shopping spree." At that time, we didn't have malls in Jamaica, so going into a shopping mall with so many stores, trying on numerous outfits, and leaving the stores with multiple shopping bags was a teenager's dream come true. Of course, all the clothes that I brought from Jamaica would not work for the fall and winter seasons in Pennsylvania. I had to get coats, jackets, scarves, hats, long-sleeved shirts, and pants. A big change for me was that I would not be wearing uniforms to school, like I did throughout high school in Jamaica. I never had to think about what I wore to school because everyone wore the same thing every day. I was excited to be able to express myself through my clothes.

August 22, 1992

Hi Mommy,

I am o.k. and really excited to be in America. I enjoyed myself in Washington D.C. and you would not imagine how nice it was to sleep in a hotel room. They give you cute little shampoos and lotions to use. There are a lot of tall buildings in this place that I've never seen in my life. The family I'm staying with is really nice. I feel at home here Aunt Bev and Uncle Jim are extremely nice too. They had a Jamaican flag at their house to make me feel welcome. Their house is so big; it's probably two times the size of our house and only four people live there. Shopping was so much fun. They have this huge place they call a mall with lots of different kinds of stores all in one place, even stores that sell food to eat. There are so many things I want to tell you, but I know that it will not all hold in this letter. I've been to McCaskey, and it is a huge, but beautiful school. Please give Carey and Dwayne a hug for me and tell Paula hello for me and that I will write to her soon. The food here is different and while I'm having fun trying these things, I really miss your cooking and the seasoning you use to make our food taste so good. You wouldn't imagine the things I'm eating. Already I'm on a diet. They are big on diets here. For lunch, I have things like a salad between low-calorie bread, low-fat milk, and fruit with some yogurt. Here they hardly eat fattening food, and it doesn't taste too bad sometimes. I am so excited that school will start soon, and I have to get everything ready since I have to wear a different outfit every day. Can you believe I won't be wearing uniforms? I miss you already!

Love
Sidoney

Saying goodbye to Godmom that first time was probably one of the hardest things I've ever done. At the back of my mind, I knew she would be leaving me at some point and I would be on my own, but when that day came, it was a lot harder than I thought. Thoughts running through my head centered on: *What if something goes wrong? I can't just get on a plane at the drop of a hat. There is a telephone, but I can't be a bother and run up an international phone bill.* As long as she was with me, I felt totally fine. When she left, I was nervous and excited all at the same time—nervous about going to a new school, nervous about how I would fit into this American family, and nervous if I could accomplish my dreams.

So, what were my dreams at that time? I wanted to go to college, get a degree, and one day work in the media as a reporter. Spending 12th grade in the U.S. was a start in the right direction. But how would I get from 12th grade to college? I didn't know, but what I did know was that I would work as hard as I could to excel in school and work my way from there.

Life Lessons From This Chapter:

- Don't be defined by your circumstances; fight for what you want.

- Don't let a setback stop you—a setback is an opportunity for a comeback.

- Know who you are and what defines you.

- Life is not fair, and you may experience racism, classism, or whatever "ism", but how you deal with it is what is important.

- Never give up hope—trust in God, and He will always work it out.

CHAPTER 2

MY POWER UNLEASHED

"It doesn't matter who you are, where you come from. The ability to triumph begins with you—always."

—Oprah Winfrey

The U.S. is a melting pot that opens its doors to people of all nations and backgrounds. The criteria may vary though, depending on the country an immigrant is from, and it's increasingly more difficult for Black and Brown immigrants. The first step in achieving the American dream is getting an education. For immigrants, that is not a luxury, but a necessity. Immigrants who are educated have a lot more opportunities than those who are not. To break down the barriers that foreigners experience, an advanced education is critical. Initially, I had no idea how I would accomplish my goals, but I had a good start. Surprisingly, this dark-skinned Jamaican had a white support system comprised of my Godmother Kathryn, her parents Grandma and Grandpa Davies, her brother Jim and his wife Doris, and the families who opened their doors to me. This had a huge impact on what I was able to achieve. My introduction to the American school system occurred in 12th grade in high school.

I was on a path to accomplishing some major goals that I set out for myself. Education has always been an important factor in my life. As a little girl growing up in Jamaica, I had dreams of going to a university and getting a degree. Having such a dream required focus, dedication, and drive. No one in my family had a college education, and I was determined to break that cycle. Leaving Jamaica as a teenager and coming to the U.S. to pursue my dream was not an easy achievement, but I did it.

Everything about my American high school was different from my high school experience in Jamaica. The biggest change was the fact that I did not wear a uniform to school. School clothes in the U.S. consisted of whatever people wanted to wear. In Jamaica, all schoolchildren wore a uniform from elementary through high school. In fact, you could identify which school a child attended by looking at the uniform.

On my first day of school, I was extremely nervous. I received my schedule, and I had to move around all over the building to get from one class to another. This was no easy task with a school the size of what to me looked like a university. My school, JP McCaskey High School located in Lancaster, Pennsylvania, was my introduction to the American education system. Another aspect of the school that was different from my Jamaican experience was that there was no devotion to start the school day. Instead, we stood and recited the Pledge of Allegiance, something I had to study and memorize because it was a requirement to recite this every morning. I leaned over to the girl beside me and asked her when we would have devotion. I chuckle at this memory because she looked at me like I had two heads and replied, "We don't do that here."

Coming from an all-girls Catholic High School to a coed school took some adjustment. The mix of boys in my school changed the learning dynamics. I noticed how distracting it was at times, but I learned quickly to fit in with the other students in my blue-jeans-and-t-shirt school attire. As I looked around, I missed my uniform because I quickly realized that this looked more like a fashion runway than a school. In fact, I was shocked by some of the clothes that I saw students wore in school. Some items, such as short shorts, would be something that I would wear to the beach and not to school. Some of the girls looked practically naked. I was glad to see that McCaskey was a diverse school, similar to what I experienced at my high school in Jamaica. There were Caucasians, African Americans, Puerto Ricans, and some international students sprinkled in the mix.

The most shocking feature I observed at my new school was the fact that there were pregnant girls at the school with the rest of us. That was unheard of in Jamaica. In Jamaica, if a girl got pregnant in high school, she either dropped out or she was sent to a "special" school with other girls who were also expectant mothers. There were several girls in my school in various stages of pregnancy. In fact, I learned that the pregnant teenagers stayed in school right up to the time they delivered their babies. In addition, to make it easier for pregnant teenage moms to return to school, there was also a daycare in our school, where the babies and young children were housed each day while their mothers attended classes. While this was shocking for me, I applaud the American school system for ensuring that everyone received an education. The convenience gave these young ladies an opportunity to continue their education and not become high school dropouts. Not completing high school would hinder their chances of moving forward in society.

The first courses I took in high school were English Literature, Geometry, American Government, Psychology, U.S. Culture, Word Processing, and Jewelry Making. I enjoyed my U.S. Culture class, as it was a good introduction to my new country.

My most challenging class was American Government. All the materials were foreign to me. Being in 12th grade, my classmates had years of learning this material, whereas I was hearing it for the first time. I had to study hard to get good grades in that class. The good news was that the subject matter was interesting and helped me understand the society that I was now calling home. No surprise that English Literature was my favorite subject. I love the fact that I was reading Shakespeare since literature had always been a favorite of mine. I loved reading books and analyzing and writing papers.

I also learned quickly that the way of teaching and test-taking in the American school system was very different from the British school system that we have in Jamaica. Multiple-choice testing is a staple in the U.S. school system but not as much in the Jamaican school system. What I grew to love most were the vast and intense discussions we had in my classes about the subjects we were learning. The teachers cared about our opinions and encouraged us to think deeply, challenge materials, and speak up. In Jamaica, we studied a great deal and took many tests, without much discussion. Since I was thriving in this new school system, all my fears of failure were unwarranted, but anyone who knows me is aware that I love to push myself to the limit.

2 Hillcrest Road
Lancaster, PA 17603
U.S.A..
October 5, 1992

Hi Mommy,

How are you doing? It's starting to get cold here and I'm not sure I like cold weather, actually, I think I hate cold weather. Everyone keeps telling me that it's going to get a lot colder.

School is going well, and I'm starting to make some friends with some of the other international students and some of the American students. We have a big event coming up at school. It's called homecoming, and all the international students will be participating in the homecoming court. It's kind of hard to explain, but I'm going to try. They have a sport here called football, but it's not like our football. They call that soccer here. The American football is almost like rugby. So, my school will play another school and halfway through the game, they crown a king and a queen who are students nominated and voted by the students. All the international students will be paired up—males and females. My "date" is a guy from Yugoslavia name Pragado, but his name is hard to pronounce so everybody calls him Pretzel. It's funny that we call him that because pretzel is a snack that is popular here. After the football game, we have a dance at school. It's coming up in a couple of weeks, and it's all that everyone is talking about. I'm excited because I'm going to have to go shopping to get a nice outfit. I will make sure to send you a picture. I miss you guys so much, and now I'm starting to miss the beautiful sunshine in Jamaica. There is practically no sun right now. Say hi to everyone for me.

Love Sidoney

I spent my first five months in the country living with Joe and Sally, then I transitioned to living with Bev and Jim, whom I affectionately began calling Aunt Bev and Uncle Jim. They were in their 70s and retired, so they had the time to devote to me. I was an "only child" for the first time in my life, and I loved it. It was nice to have all their time devoted to me. Aunt Bev spent a lot of time taking me places, exposing me to the American culture. I taught her about Jamaica, and she taught me about America. Since she's a former teacher, I was in good hands. She was very patient and answered all my questions. Oh, I had a lot of questions. Thank God, Aunt Bev was a patient person. She encouraged me to try new activities to broaden my horizon.

I decided to come out of my comfort zone and embrace what was an amazing year, not only for my academic career but also for my personal growth and development. I was a nerdy introvert who preferred to be in a corner reading a book instead of being out and about mingling with people. I decided during my 12th grade that this was a time to try something different.
I found myself raising my hand in classes and expressing myself more than I ever did during high school in Jamaica. When I began exploring what after-school activities to get involved in, I examined what I was good at, what I enjoyed doing, and what would stretch me out of my comfort zone. There were endless possibilities. There were so many after-school activities that there was something for everyone. I joined a variety of groups, namely: the Student Council; the Bible Club; the Speech and Debate Club; the American Field Service (AFS), an international youth exchange organization; and the Gospel Choir.

I enjoyed the Gospel Choir, AFS, and the Speech and Debate Club the most. AFS gave me the opportunity to become involved with the other International students. We shared our ideas about America and all the new things we were learning. Even though we were all from different parts of the world, including Brazil, Germany, Croatia, just to name a few, we all shared something similar: We were in a foreign land, learning new and exciting things. I came to rely on my new friends as we navigated a new school and culture together.

I loved to sing, so the Gospel Choir was very appealing, and it was one of my best decisions. I made many friends and was exposed to different people and places because the choir traveled all over the area and even out of state. We performed at our school, local churches, and events. I loved when we performed at multicultural churches because the congregations were predominantly Black and Hispanic and closely resembled the churches I attended back home in Jamaica. Singing in these churches was such a treat, being different from the Methodist church that I attended with Aunt Bev and Uncle Jim. I just found that it was hard for me to get engaged in the service with the hymns that I had never heard of and with the preaching that I couldn't relate to. I know that you can worship God anywhere, and I made the best of the situation. But I think the foot-stomping, handclapping, Holy-Ghost-filled churches were more to my liking. I took Aunt Bev and Uncle Jim with me to one of the choir's performances, and that shed some light on them about the church environment I grew up in. They had a greater appreciation for how much I had to adapt to their church because it was so different. I'm not sure if it was just the different religions, Methodist versus Baptist, or the makeup of the congregation that made these churches so different.

1512 Hillcrest Road
Lancaster, PA 17603
U.S.A.
November 11, 1992

Hi Godmom,

How are you doing? From your letter you sound pretty excited to be a "Movie Star." Homecoming was really exciting, and Pretzel was a total gentleman. Actually, we are good friends. We played pool together, and he made a deal that if I get better at pool, then he will get better at English. We ride our bikes together, but that cannot be done much because it's so cold. Saturday morning, we had a little snow. It wasn't a lot to see, but I could see it trickling down from the sky. Here, rap music is the in thing, and I hate it. Actually, most of the exchange students hate it, but they played a few reggae songs, and I *showed the exchange students what I know. We mostly danced to the soul (soft) songs. What was strange was people kept looking at Pretzel and me because we look so weird together. When I took off my shoes (everyone did), I looked like a little midget beside a giant. I am involved at school, and I really like it. The marking period ended yesterday, so I will be getting a report card in two weeks. Actually, it isn't hard at all to get around McCaskey. It does look big from the outside, but once you know where you are going, it's o.k. The Gospel Choir is the nicest thing that I could have joined. There are 69 members right now, and I just paid my $20 for my shirt. (All the ladies are going to get the same shirt). We went to Ebenezer Baptist, and we sang two songs. We were wonderful, and they asked us to come again. Aunt Bev + Uncle Jim was there so the next time you talk to her, ask her about it. We have a lot of engagements coming up: Saturday, November 14, Nov. 17, 20, 21, 29. Isn't that a lot. Mr. Scott told us today at practice that we will be going to Florida next spring...*

I Love and miss you
Sidoney

The Gospel Choir performed in many competitions, and the one that was most rewarding and fun-filled was our trip to Disney. This was my first time to visit Florida and Disney. It was amazing. With all the rides, food, and activities, there was so much to do. The highlight of that trip was when we spotted Michael Jackson in the park. Of course, we all went crazy at that point. That was a trip to remember and my very first vacation.

What I learned from my experience with the gospel choir was the importance of strong leadership. Mr. Scott, the teacher who led the choir, was instrumental in the success of the students in the choir. He taught us to put our all in everything that we did, as he stressed the importance of hard work, focus, and dedication. The gospel choir was primarily made up of minority students, and Mr. Scott prided himself in being a role model to us, emphasizing the importance of getting an education.

As a student. I have always felt comfortable speaking in front of large crowds. In Jamaica, I was actively involved in my church, and I constantly performed: reciting poetry, reading parts of the Bible, and singing in front of others. I decided to test those abilities when I joined the debate team. At first, I didn't even know what a debate team did, but after attending the introductory meeting, I was hooked. Basically, all my informal public speaking training served me well as a member of the debate team. To learn the inner workings of debating, I practiced tirelessly, watching the experienced debaters in my club and taking tips from them.

My first debate competition was in November 1992 in Philadelphia, and it was beyond nerve-wracking. The debaters were given a topic, one person assigned for the issue and the other candidate against it. We were given time to prepare our arguments. We each had to present them, and then the judges picked a winner. I didn't win that first contest, but I walked away feeling proud of my ability to come up with some strong arguments to defend my position. For someone who had never competed before, I did well, although my opponent beat me by a slim margin. After that first debate, I was determined to work hard and to improve each time. Soon the teacher-advisors of the club noticed and began coaching me. Yes, there was a strong Jamaican accent and sometimes I pronounced some words with a slight difference from my American counterparts, but I didn't let any of that stop me or slow my progress.

As a debater, I was successful, winning several competitions where I placed first, second, or third. While I was having fun, I never forgot my goal. Always at the back of my mind was the goal I set for myself, to ensure that after one year I would successfully land in an American college. Because of my successes in debating, I kept advancing, and I had the opportunity to travel with the debate team to various locations inside and outside of Pennsylvania. The Gospel Choir and Debate Team provided exposure and the ability to see different parts of the United States. As I began to think about college, my participation also exposed me to different college campuses. My favorite trip with the Debate Team was a visit to Harvard University for a debate competition. During that weekend at Harvard, the other debaters and I had an opportunity to tour the university, speak to admissions officers, and experience life as a student of that institution. What I remember the most about that experience was feeling how "stuffy" the campus seemed and how bitter cold it was in Boston. I hate cold weather. Although Lancaster was cold, I felt that Boston was colder, and I decided that I had no interest in applying to Harvard. Looking back on the decision-making factor of my 17-year-old self, perhaps my rationale was not logical, but at the time those were key factors for me. I did well at that Harvard competition. The competition was stiff, so walking away with third place was a great accomplishment. Looking at how far I had come was something I was most proud of. I pushed myself out of my comfort zone, and I excelled.

For the first time in my life, I had a social life! I had friends come over to my house, and I visited the homes of my friends for birthday parties or just to hang out. I participated in numerous social school activities as well. I was part of the homecoming parade, and I also participated in International Day, which was fun. Students represented the country they or their parents were from. Marlon, Harlon, Fabian, and I represented Jamaica. Aunt Bev helped me cook jerk chicken, rice and beans, and other Jamaican food as well. We also had to do an activity that represented our culture. We did a reggae dance. I recruited my African American friend, Shaniqua, and she recruited one of her girlfriends. We taught them the dance routine for the song. We performed the dance, which was such a hit, and I enjoyed showcasing my culture.

The experience I had at home was vastly different from the one I had at school, and I was learning to juggle both worlds. After arriving in the United States, I noticed the emphasis placed on race. When I was with my host family and their upper-middle-class friends and acquaintances, I became an anomaly. Many had never interacted so closely with someone who was Black. People were curious and asked many strange questions about Jamaica as well as personal questions about me. People wanted to touch my hair, asked me what products I used on my skin, and if people lived in hut houses in Jamaica. At school there was another experience. While I attended a diverse school, many of the groups predominantly associated with people from their race—the Black students almost exclusively associated with each other, likewise the White and Latino students. For me, being from a place where mixed races were used to interacting with each other, it took a bit of getting accustomed to this norm, but I found myself floating through various groups.

The intense focus on race was the most difficult change for me as an immigrant in the U.S. People are defined by their race. Every form that you fill out asks whether you are Black, White, Hispanic, Native American, etc. Everywhere I went, people took the time to tell me that I was Black. I received these comments from both Black and White people, and it had me shaking my head as to why it was even necessary to mention my race. I found this to be strange because we don't do that in Jamaica. People don't ask if you are White Jamaican, Chinese Jamaican, or Black Jamaican; we are all just Jamaicans. But as a result, I found myself looking more in the mirror, noticing the dark shade of my skin, the kinkiness of my hair, and the strong features of my nose and mouth. Because of my environment, I found myself focusing more on race. I would analyze it when someone walked behind me and followed me around in the store when I went to the mall. *Are they doing that because I'm Black?* I kept mulling over these thoughts in my head. I experienced all this while trying to juggle all the adjustments of living in a new country. While I dealt with these new realities, I didn't lose sight of my focus to ensure that my education was my topmost priority.

1512 Hillcrest Road
Lancaster, PA 17603
U.S.A.
December 7, 1992

Hi Mommy,

So much has happened since my last letter. I'm settling in alright, and school is going well and I'm passing my classes. American government is kind of hard. I've been here three months and it is the strangest thing, but here in America, everyone tells me that I'm Black as if I don't look in the mirror. People here are hung up on race, and it's mentioned all the time. People ask me the strangest things, and it's especially strange when they ask to touch my hair. I miss home a lot now that it is extremely cold; I am never going to complain about the sun ever again. Here, it feels like when you stick your head in a freezer, and it is like that all the time when you go outside. Even with a coat on, I'm always freezing. I had an ice-skating party for my birthday. A lot of my friends from school were there. My party went o.k. Actually, by the end of the night, I was ice skating all by myself. I had the most wonderful teacher, my new "boyfriend". He is 10 years old and he adopted me for the night. He is an ice hockey player. We returned to my house and we had lasagna, chips, sodas, you name it. We had a lot of fun dancing, listening to music, and playing pool. I miss spending my birthday with you guys, but it was still good. Please write me and let me know how my brothers are doing. I miss you Mommy, and I hope you're taking care of yourself.

Love Always,
Sidoney

High school was not all about fun and games. The first step to getting into one of the American colleges or universities was to take the Scholastic Aptitude Test (SAT). I had no idea what the SAT was. I went to the library and got a book about SATs, but that was the extent of my preparation. I sat for the SAT for the first time thinking I was smart so I should do well on this American exam. I was confident that since my classes weren't that difficult and I was getting almost all A's, I would be fine. Boy, was I wrong! What I failed to recognize was that I was from a totally different school system, a system that taught differently and did not rely heavily on multiple-choice questions. In Jamaica, you wrote essays to explain most things. I bombed the SAT the first time around.

I remember sitting at the dinner table when my results came back. Aunt Bev explained to me that if I wanted to get into college, the score I got wouldn't do it. I was disappointed. I don't give up easily, so I looked at this as a short setback. Fortunately, I had Aunt Bev as my patient teacher. She had a Bachelor of Science degree, majoring in Physical Education, English, and Science. Aunt Bev also taught in the Lancaster School District for 10 years, so I knew I was in great hands. I studied and did practice tests repeatedly. Aunt Bev quizzed me, corrected my tests, and showed me what I could improve on. I started doing better. I was now getting more things correct than wrong. I adapted to the multiple-choice exams and learned how to work on them quickly and accurately. After a few months, I retook the SAT and—*voila!*—I earned a great score. Aunt Bev was so proud. She told me that this score would not only get me into college, but it could also help me get a scholarship, which is the only way I could afford to go to an American college.

Getting into college is not for the faint at heart. Most of my friends who were seniors already knew where they were going to college. They had done their SAT in their junior year and had applied to numerous schools, so for them, it was just a matter of waiting. I, on the other hand, was starting from ground zero. Passing the SAT was only the first of many steps. I had to decide which schools I wanted to apply to and what I wanted to study. Once I decided on which colleges to apply to, I then had to complete the applications, which is like a class in and of itself. Each school had its own criteria as to what they wanted to be included. I was fortunate to have Aunt Bev who guided me throughout the process.

The most difficult part of the application process was the essay. You had to tell each school why you were applying to their school and why they should accept you. I labored over my essays because I wanted to get them right. Getting my thoughts on paper was not difficult, but I had to answer the question "Why should these Americans let me into their schools when I had no money to pay?" Surely, they could get students whose parents could pay for them to attend. However, I didn't let that stop me. I explained what a college education would mean for this girl from the ghettos of Kingston, Jamaica. It would be a dream come true. I would be the first one in my family to have a college degree, and that would be a significant accomplishment that could set me on the path to something more than I had growing up. The second part was to convince them that I had something to offer, to show them what I could bring to their institution. Being from Jamaica, I offered a different perspective which I thought was unique; I brought my cultural background as well as my tenacity and ability to work hard and excel. Those were critical components I included in my college essays. And it worked.

I decided that I didn't want to go to a college that would be too far from the only support system I had in the United States. I looked at several schools in Pennsylvania: Millersville University, Franklin and Marshall College, Lebanon Valley College, and Grove City College. After I identified the schools, Aunt Bev and Uncle Jim took me on college visits to all the schools. During those visits, I toured the schools and met with the admissions and financial aid officers.

The most beneficial part was the meeting with current students who shared how they liked the school, both the academic program as well as the ambiance of college life. After those visits, I decided to apply to Lebanon Valley College, Elizabethtown College, and Grove City College. I sent in all my documents—application, financial aid information, letters of recommendation, high school transcript—and then I sat and waited.

When I started getting involved in school activities, I didn't even know that these things would help me when it was time to apply for college. Aunt Bev suggested I have my essays include all the activities that I was involved in. She had me write about joining the debate team and the numerous awards that I received. Since I knew I wanted to major in communications, I decided to include my first published article as part of my college application. This, I believed, would show what I had to offer and differentiate me from the other applicants. The local newspaper, *The Lancaster Intelligencer,* ran an annual competition where students from first through twelve grades could submit an article on a topic of their choice. The newspaper chose one winner for each grade, and that student's article and photo appeared in the newspaper. I won the 12th Grade spot for my article "Justice for All," making it my first published article.

12th Grade Winner
'Justice for All'
Sidoney Samuels
Grade 12
McCaskey HS

"Whops," "Spiks," "Niggers," and "Homo,"—these names have been around for decades. (I just want to make you aware that prejudice exists.)

Prejudice—when I say that all too familiar word or hear it, some part of me turns off, and I imagine that it happens to you too. When we hear the word, we all feel that we know all about the topic but, because it has been around for so long, our minds tend to close down no matter how open we try to be.

The word doesn't carry through the pain, senselessness, and danger it presents to us all. People are prejudiced mainly against race, color, religion, and sexual preferences. Who are we to judge another human being? Each individual has the right to be whomever they want. We can't all be the same people. If we were, then I can't imagine what the world would be like.

The "famous" Adolf Hitler tried to make a unified world at the expense of millions of innocent people who suffered brutally, died, and the grief still continues today. Recently, Temple Beth El in Lancaster was defaced with Swastikas, symbols of the anti-Semitic Nazi Party. Being disgusted and irritable as I was with this act of prejudice, I joined other concerned citizens of the community at a special service held at the synagogue.

Let me implore you that as civilized individuals we need to stand up to people who are prejudiced toward us and others. We did not make ourselves so we shouldn't be made to suffer physical and or verbal abuse for how we are.

We've got to live together. Learn to love, cherish, understand, and respect each other for who we are. We need to realize that we are brothers and sisters, and we should learn to live in peace and harmony.

So, the next time you hear the Pledge of Allegiance "And Justice for All," ask yourself—can you afford to risk missing out on what may be a wonderful friendship, interaction, and relationship with another individual of a different race, religion, creed or belief than yourself? And, if you can answer no, then, and only then will there be some form of justice for all.

Waiting to hear from the colleges was hard. I checked the mailbox every day for a letter from my three schools. I didn't realize how much I wanted to get into college until after I sent off those applications and I was awaiting the decisions. I prayed a lot, asking God for favor that I would get into college and that He would make a way for me, financially, as well. Aunt Bev was extremely optimistic, and she reminded me how much progress I made from when I first started the process.

403 W. Orange Street
Lancaster, PA 17603
February 15, 1993

Dear Godmom,

I just got back from my Speech + Debate Tournament at Harvard University in Boston. Tell Anna that I went to her hometown. It was colder than Lancaster will ever be. Tomorrow we will have possibly 6 inches of snow. It will start falling by midnight. The colleges got my grades from

McCaskey. I'm sorry I didn't mention it. I left Lancaster at 12:15 p.m. on Thursday Feb 11. and I got to our hotel at 10:00 p.m. We left Boston at 10:00 a.m. and we arrive in Philadelphia at 6:00 p.m. and we had to wait until 9:13 p.m. to get a train to Lancaster. I know you won't approve that's why I'm telling you. While I was at the train station in Philly this guy came up to me and we began talking and guess what...I gave him my phone number. (It's o.k. you don't have to get a heart attack I gave him the wrong number). I am the 12th Grade winner for a local contest of the newspaper. I will send you a copy of the letter and certificate. No need to worry I got a relaxer perm. One of my girlfriends did it for me. It looks rather good all my friends agree.

I am going to a different church and Aunt Bev doesn't object. This one is more like my style. I came 2nd in the Pennsylvania Division Speech Tournament. My topic was "Prejudice" I have a nice trophy. I've left the best news for last. I just got a letter from Lebanon Valley and guess what? I have been accepted and throughout the course of this week, they will send me financial information. I have until May 1 to respond to them. Isn't that great now I only have E-town and Grove City to wait on.

Xoxo
Sidoney

P.S. Don't worry I won't do anything that I know you wouldn't want me to do.

I was so happy and proud that I got accepted to the three schools I applied to. I couldn't believe they wanted me. I was going to be the first person in my family to get a college education. All the way from Jamaica—my dreams were beginning to take shape. Decision-making around which college to attend can be tricky.

For me, it was simple, I would go with the school that offered me the most money. I was seeking a good liberal arts education, and all three institutions of higher learning could provide that. I decided on Elizabethtown College, a small liberal arts college in Elizabethtown, Pennsylvania. They offered me a full-tuition scholarship for all four years if I met the criteria each year for my scholarship. From what I understood, that was quite an accomplishment to receive a scholarship of that magnitude. All I needed to pay for was my room and board and books. They also told me I could work on campus for 20 hours per week to help with money. What started as a dream was coming to fruition. Perseverance paid off. Had I given up when I got that awful SAT score, I wouldn't have realized my dream.

> *403 W. Orange Street*
> *Lancaster, PA 17603*
> *June 1, 1993*

Dear Grandma Davies,

I hope you and grandpa are in the best of health. I can't be-lieve that the year has come to an end. It's very hard for me to realize how time went by quickly. I have learned a lot this year that I will cherish throughout my life. Thanks for your generosity. I received your $50, and indeed I am going to put it to good use. I put it in my college account already. Well, the Prom is this Friday, and I am extremely excited. Kathryn comes up on Saturday and on Sunday I will have a party then next Tuesday I will graduate.

> *Love Sidoney*

The two significant events that occurred towards the end of that school year were the prom and graduation. The prom was the talk of the 12th grade for several months. All the girls talked about their outfits, what they would wear, what they would not wear, where they would go out to eat before prom, whether they would get a limousine or not, what kind of music would be played, and the talk went on and on. I had never been to a prom before. In fact, prior to this, I had no idea what a prom was. I wondered why the parents would spend so much money on a one-day event. To me, it seemed like it was a "wedding" for teenagers, minus the white dress and the ring. I invited a friend of mine, Brandon, who was a junior, to go with me. I wore a beautiful off-the-shoulder black dress. Uncle Jim got all dressed up in a black suit and served as our chauffeur in his fancy car. I felt like a princess for a day. The dance was a lot of fun, and I enjoyed hanging out with friends that I made all year.

There was something so final about this experience. I realized that after these two events, I might never see some of these people again. Many classmates were going to different colleges or tech schools. None of my friends was going to Elizabethtown College. Some were not pursuing college at all and were looking for full-time jobs to help out financially at home. A few just didn't see more school in their future because they had parents and guardians who didn't attend college and couldn't provide any guidance. Many people are defined by their circumstances and their socioeconomic background. I'm glad I had people in my life who helped me rise above my socioeconomic status. There were many scholarships available for students who couldn't afford college, but they had to put in the work to seek and apply for those opportunities. Some students just don't have the support system required to push them to the next level. I consider myself blessed for the support that I experienced.

This graduation was special to me. I was asked to deliver a speech at the graduation ceremony, in front of all my classmates and their families. If someone a year prior had told me I would stand on a stage in the United States of America, delivering a speech at my graduation ceremony, I would not have believed that would be possible. From very humble beginnings, I did not take this moment lightly. In the audience, I had my support system. Mom and Godmom came up from Jamaica, and they were there along with Aunt Bev and Uncle Jim and Sally and Joe. This was my mom's first visit to the United States and the best surprise graduation present that I could have ever asked for. To celebrate my graduation, we had a party where I invited many of my friends and some of my teachers from school. It was nice just to sit back and relax. I had so much fun and couldn't have been happier.

College Bound—Higher Education, Here I Come

I did it! I entered the U.S. with dreams, aspirations, and an inner drive. As the first one in my family to go to college, I had a sense of pride, and more importantly, I had a burden to ensure that I made good use of yet another opportunity that I was blessed to have. Over the summer, I received information that my roommate was another international student from Japan. Yuka and I would be exploring college life together. I was excited, hoping we could help each other in our college transition.

In August 1993, Aunt Bev, Uncle Jim, and Godmom drove me to the dorms at Elizabethtown College, a small rural college town, fifteen minutes from Hershey Park. Aunt Bev helped me get my half of the dorm room set up and put my stuff away. There was so much to learn and understand. Uncle Jim helped me figure out my mailbox and locker combination. As we took another tour of the school, I familiarized myself with all the important places I needed to locate right away—the library, the cafeteria, the school bookstore, and my dorm. Before deciding on Elizabethtown College, I spent a weekend on campus to gain the college experience. I was paired with another student who showed me around. It was a weekend in the life of a college student minus attending classes. I'm glad I had that experience so things were not brand new on my first day. Saying goodbye this time to Godmom was much easier. I would miss her, but the year spent in the U.S. prepared me for this next chapter. Elizabethtown was about a 45-minute drive from where Aunt Bev and Uncle Jim lived, so I knew they were right around the corner if I needed them.

After everyone left, I began reflecting and came to the realization that for the first time in my life I was totally on my own. I was not under the supervision of an adult and would have to make decisions for every aspect of my life. After my family left, my roommate, Yuka, and I formally introduced ourselves. Yuka was very shy and reserved, but she had a pleasant smile, so I knew we would be okay. We talked about our dorm room, things we needed to spruce up, and we shared information about our families and countries of birth. I learned that Yuka decided to attend Elizabethtown College because her older sister was a student at nearby Franklin and Marshall College in Lancaster. I shared my senior year experience with her. I was somewhat apprehensive about sharing a room with someone I didn't know, but from the onset, I knew that Yuka and I wouldn't have any problems.

As planned, I entered college as a communications major. Declaring a major in my freshman year allowed me to take classes in the Communications and Journalism department. I took a full course load during my first semester. My courses were Writing and Language, Freshman Seminar, Introduction to Media Production, Shakespeare through Performance, Media and Society, and Soccer. College was different from high school in that you didn't go to classes every day for a consecutive number of hours. Instead, you attended classes based on your course load. Some days, I didn't have classes, so managing my time was of utmost importance.

There were no teachers in college reminding you to study, and there were no study halls, so you had to be disciplined in completing assignments and studying for tests. There was so much freedom in college, and what someone decided to do with it determined their success or failure. I decided early on that my focus would be on my studies. I got a job, working in the cafeteria 20 hours per week. All the money earned I used to pay for incidentals. Godmom paid for my room and board and covered my books. I considered myself blessed to have her in my life. I could comfortably focus on my studies and not worry about paying for college. My focus was to maintain my grade point average (GPA) so that I would qualify yearly for my full-tuition scholarship.

First Job

In Jamaica, it was not customary for teenagers to have part-time jobs, like I observed in the U.S. My first job was as a server in the cafeteria. The good thing about working on campus was the flexibility the job provided. I was able to tailor my work hours around my classes, tests, and on-campus activities and clubs. Working in the cafeteria was not a glamorous job, but it provided a paycheck, and I was grateful to secure a job. I started off serving food on the line to students who came in for meals during my shifts. I was a fast learner, so I began to pick up my tasks rather quickly. I tried to excel in everything that I did, and this was no exception. After a couple of months, I was moved up to a position that had more responsibilities. On our campus, the banquet hall in our cafeteria was rented out for events and functions, such as weddings, birthdays, and other celebrations. In addition to my job in the cafeteria, I was offered the job as a banquet server for functions. What I loved about this job was the higher pay. Between working and my courses, I had little time for much of anything else, so I had to choose my extracurricular activities wisely.

1223 Elizabethtown College
Elizabethtown, PA 17022
September 3, 1993

Dear Mommy,

I want to wish you a happy birthday. I'm sorry I'm not there to help you celebrate, but I'm sure Carey and Dwayne will make it special for you. College is everything that I thought it would be; it is hard work, but you know that I'm not afraid of hard work. I have lots and lots of reading. Sometimes I have to read up to 80 pages per night. Sometimes my roommate and I are studying until 3 o clock in the morning. My roommate is Japanese, and we seem to get along well. We both love to laugh and enjoy ourselves. There are not many "people of color" that's what they call Black people here. Out of a freshman class of almost 500, there are two of us. I don't let that bother me at all. I just call to everybody and get into the groove of things. I miss Jamaica sometimes, especially now that the cold weather will be here soon. Most of all, I miss your cooking. The food here is not always the best because they forget to add seasoning to the dishes. I go to Church on campus, it's not the same as it is in Jamaica, but I try to go as much as possible. Sometimes, I can't make it because I have to work. Working in the cafeteria is not so bad. I'm getting the hang of it. I work there three times per week. I get paid $4.40 an hour, and when I work on Fridays, I get an extra $1.00 per hour. I also have a job in the Admissions department where I talk to prospective students. I do that two days per week. I'm learning how to juggle classes with my jobs. My grades are decent, so don't worry. My number-one priority is to get good grades so that I can keep my scholarship. Say hi to everyone for me.

Love Sidoney

Unlike JP McCaskey High School, Elizabethtown College's student population was not diverse, and there were very few minority students. I joined the Black Student Union. That club served as a support system for the Black students on campus. I made some friends there, and I got involved with the step team. Stepping was a choreographed way of moving to a specific kind of music. It is immensely popular in the African American college community. I had fun learning those steps and performing at various college events. With my limited time, I made the decision that my second extracurricular activity would be something in my major. I worked as a reporter for ECTV Channel 40 News and as a disc jockey for the radio station. I had to go through training with a senior disc jockey and had to learn how to use the board, make announcements, and transition from playing to making announcements. I worked the graveyard and early morning shifts. A lot of college students don't like to get up early, but I didn't mind at all because I've always been an early riser. I took all the slots I could get because I found myself improving over time.

1223 Elizabethtown College
Elizabethtown, PA 17022-2259
U.S.A..
October 20, 1993

Dear Godmom,

It was great talking to you earlier this week. I was incredibly surprised and happy to hear your voice. I'm going to see Mommy one more time before she returns home; so, I'm looking forward to that. I did a reporting package this afternoon. It went pretty well, in my opinion. I hope the extended audience likes it. I did a presentation in my Writing and Language class, and I got an A- that made me feel rather good. My professor used my style as an example.

Sidoney Samuels-Buckridge   45

She said my posture and eye contact were excellent. I don't know how I'm going to work out my Christmas break. I have one month, and many people want me, so I have to come up with a plan. I get off school December 18 and return January 18. My uncle in Washington wants to see me. My grandmother wants me, and I want to go see Anna in Boston and, of course, Aunt Bev and Uncle Jim would like to see a little of me. I might have to choose because it's going to cost me a lot to go to all those places... I think this picture will convince you that I am still working at my computers. Actually, Elizabethtown has a very confusing system, and I have taught myself how to use it. My computer skills from McCaskey helped. I spend a lot of time in the Computer Labs. Professors don't accept handwritten work. Also, in graphics (communications) I use the computer to create designs. I want to see how much money I saved throughout the year and next summer. After I pay for school, if I have money left over, I want to buy a used computer, preferably a Mackintosh. The used ones are going for about $300. I know it's a lot, but I think it's worth it, seeing that it is used so often and would be more convenient if it was in my room. Midterms are almost over. Soon I will be choosing my courses for next year. Take care and write soon. Presently, I have been taking Black and white exposures, and I also develop them myself. Can you believe it? Write soon.

Love Sidoney

P.S. notice my hair is done!!

With all that I had going on, Yuka and I did not see much of each other. Yuka's parents paid outright for her education and provided her with a monthly stipend to cover all her incidentals. As a result, she didn't have to work. When I wasn't working, we grabbed our meals together at the cafeteria, and occasionally, we would go to a dance on campus. Yuka spent a lot of her time improving her craft, either drawing or making pottery. As I suspected, Yuka and I got along well. I heard numerous roommate horror stories, so I was thankful that we compromised and made it work.

I finished my first semester of college with a strong showing. I would have liked to see more A's on my first-semester report card, but I was still pleased with my grades:

Soccer   B+
Media & Society   B
Freshman Seminar   A-
Writing and Language   B+
Introduction to Media Production   B-
Shakespeare Through Performance   A-

I was most proud of working a part-time job and keeping my grades where they needed to be. After all, if I lost my scholarship, that would be the end of my goal of receiving a college degree. In addition, I was able to make some friends and had a little fun along the way. As we neared our final exams, I observed that this was the only time that some students decided to study. They would spend a lot of time partying and having a good time, and their courses were secondary to having fun. For me, I knew how critical a college education would be to my future, so I always kept my priorities at the forefront of my mind.

One of the benefits of college was getting a month off for Christmas break. I was happy for the break, and I went home to Aunt Bev and Uncle Jim and did a lot of sleeping. It was a time to lounge around, and I connected with some of my high school friends who were also home from college. It was good to swap stories about our college experiences. I was looking forward to the second semester in a new dorm. Yuka and I were originally in Founders Dorm in a tiny room. When the opportunity opened up to move into another dorm with a loft, we jumped on it. The second semester was a lot easier than the first. I had a mix of courses in both my major and core courses. I knew my way around campus and was better able to balance my courses with my part-time job. I had a few friends I hung out with and enjoyed my extracurricular activities.

> *1223 Elizabethtown College*
> *Elizabethtown, PA 17022-2259*
> *U.S.A.*
> *February 4, 1994*

Dear Godmom,

I hope you are doing o.k. The weather is really terrible here. Enjoy the sunshine for both of us. Last week I had an asthma attack. I developed a cold and that triggered off things. I got two days off from classes. I took one of the days off and I made my way to classes the other. My new dorm is really nice. We have much more space than at Founders. The girls have been nice to us so far. The first week we were here they all came over and chatted with us for a while. Something we didn't experience in Founders. When good programs are on television, they even invite us over. We are comfortable. I was just helping Yuka write her personal essay for her application to the Pennsylvania School of Art and Design. I know that I'm going to miss her a lot. I know people in Jamaica think that America is heaven and that everything here is like paradise. But we both know that it is not like that anywhere in the world. It's good to be in shape for health reasons and, of course, to show off the beautiful body (smile). I work out three times per week, so I have joined you guys. A big difference though because I can't be outside. The body shop is the place to be. Lucky you, I wouldn't mind travelling the world like you do. Have fun in Australia. Classes are going o.k. so far. I won't give much of an opinion because I haven't taken any test or exam yet. My religion class is weird. This guy lights candles and talks about mystical whatever? I hope I survive. I'm not sure if I will be working for ECTV this semester because this is my first semester of being a manager, and I am not sure if I can handle it. I want to see how things work out first. I finally got my eyes checked. I did it on my own because I just couldn't wait for Aunt Bev and Uncle Jim and things got worse. I went to State Optical in Park City. One of my friends told me that she recommends them highly. The doctor said that I have astigmatism. My eye exam and glasses cost me $120 that I took it out of the account I have for myself. I'm not sure what Aunt Bev and Uncle Jim's reaction will be. The fact that I did it on my own. When that milestone comes, I will cross it. I just feel that I am old enough to start taking responsibility for things that concern me. What do you think? I spoke to Mommy the other day, and she told me that she is thinking of coming to see me this summer and if at all possible, she will try and bring Dwayne along. You can just imagine that I got excited. I hope it will work out. I also hope to see you this summer. Are you still planning to come? If so, write and tell me when. My friend and I were looking at schools where we think we would like to pursue a master's degree. I sent away for some information on some universities. One thing I am sure of is that I don't think I want another place as dull as E-town. I hope you are making progress in your packing. I wish I could come and help you. But we both know that is impossible. (I would be coming for the warmth more than anything else.

I can't wait for SPRING!). I finally met Doris. I like her because she is full of life and natural. Doris offered to have me stay at her house for Spring Break (Aunt Bev will be on vacation). I didn't give her an answer because I am not sure

Sidoney Samuels-Buckridge   49

what I will be doing. I think I will go to Washington for a week. It gets kind of dull in Lancaster. I think I have told you everything that's happening. Say hello to everybody for me.

Love Sidoney

I successfully finished my first year of college and qualified for my sophomore year scholarship. I was pleased with my results and happy that I was one step closer towards my goal of achieving higher education. I was also pleased during my sophomore year that I was able to secure a job that provided a lot of benefits. I got a resident assistant (RA) job. The greatest benefit of this job was the free room and board along with a monthly stipend. This was great news for Godmom, who no longer had to pay for room and board. Essentially, I would be getting a totally free education! In addition, I secured a job for the summer, working as a banquet manager in the school cafeteria. Per the conditions of my student visa, during the summer months, I could work full-time (40 hours). This was great because I was able to make more spending money over the summer.

Since I was staying on campus during the summer, I decided to take one summer course. I figured, "Why not knock out some of these courses?" It was lonely on campus during the summer, and this would help me pass the time. The vibrant, bursting campus that exists during the school year was absent. Some international students went home to their countries, and very few remained on campus. Besides working and studying for my class, I took the time to relax and catch up on my reading. During the school year, I didn't get to do much reading for fun. I spent my time juggling my courses, part-time job, and extracurricular activities. So, it was nice to go to the library, grab a novel, and curl up with it.

I loved sharing my college experience with my younger brother, Dwayne. He was only seven years old when I left Jamaica, so my relationship with him was different from my relationship with Carey. The bulk of our relationship was remote: writing letters, talking on the phone, and connecting on my visits to Jamaica. I wanted to play a big role in his life, hoping that I would pave the way and that he would follow my example and migrate to the U.S. to get a college education.

During the summer after my freshman year, my mom and 10-year-old brother Dwayne came for a visit. It was Dwayne's first visit to the U.S., and he was beyond excited. Mom spent a week with me before moving on to New York to spend time with friends. I gave them a tour of the campus, and she also got a chance to meet the president of the college, Dr. Spiegel. The highlight of the visit was a day-long trip to nearby Hershey Park. Dwayne had the time of his life on all the rides, especially the water rides. This theme park is unlike anything that existed in Jamaica, so when I planned the trip, I knew he would have fun. He enjoyed eating all the cotton candy, pizza, and junk food he could get his hands on. I spent some time encouraging Dwayne to do well in school so that he could one day end up on a college campus like the one I was attending. It was good to spend some time with my mom and younger brother.

At the end of the summer, I joined all the other RAs on campus for training. We received information about our roles and responsibilities, expectations of the job, and our dorm assignments. We participated in team-building activities and scenario role-playing. Senior RAs were paired with incoming RAs to share their experiences and provide successful tips. I was assigned to Schlosser Residence Hall, an all-female dorm.

At the start of my sophomore year, I was happy to be in my own room and excited to take on the challenge of my new role as an RA. What exactly is an RA? RAs help students get situated to life in a college dorm and enhance their on-campus experience. RAs assist fellow residents with personal and educational matters while also fostering a sense of community. My job was to work with the residents on my floor by planning activities and providing a safe environment for all students under my watch.

Below were some of my RA responsibilities:

- Assist with Welcome Week activities, including opening dorms, checking students in, and ensuring student participation.

- Staff the RA station and be on-call to handle issues that arise.

- Check dorm rooms for infractions or safety issues and submit reports on any violations of college rules.

- Enforce college rules and regulations while acting as a bridge between students and the college administration.

- Assist students with specific needs and make referrals when they are beyond my ability to handle.

- Plan activities to build a sense of community in the dorm.

- Organize floor meetings with residents on a regular basis.

- Moderate disagreements between students, residents, and fellow resident assistants.

- Provide information about on-campus activities and events and campus initiatives.

I learned a lot from being an RA. I developed leadership and negotiation skills I didn't even know I had. I was resolving conflicts between roommates, handling the homesickness of residents, and helping with relationship issues. I also had to plan exciting events that would keep the young ladies engaged so that they would attend. As an RA, I discovered I was a friend, confidante, counselor, and administrator, all wrapped up into one. This job was not as easy as I initially thought. I found that the residents had conflicts at very inconvenient times for me—when I was studying for a test or had a deadline in one of my courses. I couldn't turn them away, so I had to rely on my time-management and planning skills to help me manage the job with my academics and my extracurricular activities. My life was a constant juggling act. During my sophomore year, I was also a feature writer for the school's newspaper, *The Etownian,* where my first feature story appeared on September 15, 1995. It was about a new professor who joined the Fine and Performing Arts Department on campus.

1223 Elizabethtown College
Elizabethtown, PA 17022
September 17, 1995

Dear Godmom,

How are you? I hope that you are having fun on your vacation. Jay (Godmom's husband) *told me that you will be visiting your parents, so I thought you would get the letter quicker. School is going all right, and I am doing O.K. I am really excited because my first feature story came out in the paper on Friday. Enclosed is a copy. Tell me what you honestly think. Another excitement!! My friends and I went to see Boyz II Men live on Thursday. We had the time of our lives. My hall is doing o.k. I had a picnic last week and the attendance was great. On the 26th of this month we will be*

*having a Condom Party. Don't be alarmed, let me explain.
A Condom Party is given by the Wellness Peer Educators in
conjunction with the health center. The purpose is to present
the option of birth control to the residents. No one is forced
or coerced. They present the different types of birth control
methods, and we also have fun by playing: Pin the Condom
on the man and who is the fastest to put the condom
correctly on the cucumber. I am also enclosing some pictures
that I took while my Mom and Dwayne were here. I started
the application process for the semester in Washington.
Now I have to wait until I hear from them. I am thinking
of sending away for graduate school information. Do you
have any particular school in mind that I should be looking
at? Aunt Bev and Uncle Jim will be coming up for Parent's
Weekend. I think that will be fun to spend a little time with
them. Also, for Fall Break I will be staying at my best friend's
house in Scranton, P.A. So, I'm anxious about that. Did Anna
get a job? Do you know her address? I would love to get in
touch with her. Did you get my tape about my audio essay
and paper? Did you like it? Let me know. Well, I have to go,
so take care and write soon.*

*Love always
Sidoney*

I finished my sophomore year strong and qualified for my
junior year scholarship. In addition, I would serve as an RA
for a second year. I would again receive free room and board.
For the summer, I secured an on-campus full-time job in the
College Relations Department, where I would be working in my
field and getting practical experience doing public relations.
This involved doing office work, keeping track of media clips
where the college is featured, and forwarding media calls to
the appropriate person. As a communications major with a double
concentration in journalism and public relations, there were so

many avenues someone could go in the communications field, so doing a double concentration would provide more options for me in the future. Because of my work in this department, I was given the opportunity to write my first feature story in the college magazine sent to alumni. There was no point in sitting around campus during the summer, so I used the opportunity to take another college course.

My junior year was the year of reality for me. I was that much closer to achieving my dream of obtaining a college degree. I had to make an important decision about my academic career. I had a meeting with my academic advisor, who informed me that since I took summer courses, I had enough credits to graduate in December of my senior year. Of course, I told him no. Not many students wanted to graduate in December because you don't get a chance to attend the big graduation ceremony. He explained my options: either graduate, study abroad, or spend a semester in the Washington D.C. Semester Program. I decided to apply for the Washington Semester Program. The good news was that my tuition scholarship from Elizabethtown could be transferred to American University, where the program was held. All I needed to cover was room and board. I applied and was accepted into the Washington Semester Program.

Serving as an RA my second year was much easier. I made some adjustments, and my time management skills improved. I also continued to write for *The Etownian* as a feature writer. Throughout college, I slowly built up my communications portfolio, which was especially important during my senior year when I applied to graduate schools. As an upperclassman, the bulk of my courses were in the Communications School, including Advanced Public Relations, Video Production, Broadcast News and Copywriting, and Junior/Senior Colloquium: America through Foreign Eyes. As always, my focus was to ensure that I continued to get good grades. This program, therefore, was even more attractive because not only would I be attending classes at American University, but I would also be spending a considerable amount of time getting practical experience working for a newspaper as an intern, which I could add to my portfolio.

I finished my junior year strong and qualified for my senior year scholarship. When I received the letter informing me that I had qualified for my scholarship, I felt like I was running a marathon and being on the last lap, so this letter meant so much more than all the others. When the school year came to an end, I spent one month in Jamaica. What I enjoyed the most about being back home was the delicious Jamaican food that I could always have: the spicy jerk chicken, the juicy mangoes, and not to mention beef patty and coco bread. I made sure that I savored every moment eating these foods that I couldn't get in America. My favorite pastime was enjoying the clear blue waters of the Caribbean Sea. Having been to Rehoboth Beach in Delaware and the Ocean City Maryland beach in the U.S., I had a greater appreciation for the white sandy beaches that many Jamaicans take for granted. I also spent most of my time that month working in my church. It was good to get back to church being a constant in my life. Attending Mass on campus is not the same as attending Mass in Jamaica, where we have tambourines and drums going at all of our services.

I returned to Jamaica a week before Christ The King Catholic Church's Annual Jamaica Night Barbecue celebration. As part of the barbecue event, there was an entertainment portion, and they were looking for someone to help two youth groups coordinate a dance routine. I stepped up to the task and taught the preteens and the 16-to-18-year-old age groups. My younger brother Dwayne was in the preteen dance group. The productions turned out well. In addition, I also served as the Mistress of Ceremonies for the event—putting my nearly completed communications degree to the test. I also spent time connecting with my mom and hanging out with friends Stacia, Nicole, and Trisha from Holy Childhood High School.

I had an interesting encounter with the nun who was the meanest to me when I was at boarding school. I returned to the boarding school for a visit. I saw the den mother, who gave me a big hug, and I also saw the nun who so many years ago made me feel like I didn't belong. The encounter with her took a 180-degree turn. Of course, she asked what I was doing with myself, and I was proud to report that I was entering my last year of college. I gladly informed her of my accomplishments: staff writer for the newspaper with weekly published articles, disc jockey for the radio station, dean's list awardee, and a full-tuition scholarship recipient for all four years of college. Her response shocked me. She told me she always knew I had it in me to do well. Since she is a woman of God, I know that I should believe her, but I didn't. I think she and I both knew how she treated me, and she was trying to save face. I was glad that I could prove her wrong and a small part of me hoped that the encounter with me would help her think twice about judging people and using her biases to categorize others.

When I returned from Jamaica, I went to my full-time summer job, working in the College Relations Department for the second summer. Many changes occurred in that department during that time. Our college president, Dr. Spiegler, was retiring, and our new president, Dr. Long, took the reins. The College Relations Department was also experiencing changes. The head of our department also retired, and his next-in-command who handled the college magazine took over. Amidst the changes, I got the opportunity to see the inner workings of a public relations department. We had a press conference to introduce the new college president. I was given the chance to contribute to the press release, work on the media list, and help on the day of the press conference. I felt fortunate to be given this opportunity. Throughout my college career, I always thought I would go into journalism and work as a reporter, but I also found the public relations side of the field was also interesting.

1223 Elizabethtown College
Elizabethtown, PA 17022
U.S.A..
July 21, 1996

Dear Godmom,

I was happy when I received your letter. It's really sad that Debra Lee and Jennifer will no longer be a part of the Special Olympics gang. I was actually looking forward to seeing Jennifer when I'm in Washington. I know that you will really miss Jennifer. Will Debra Lee remain in Jamaica? Will someone replace her? I checked my email, and I didn't receive one from you. I will send a message to the last email address that I have for Jay.

I just got back from Ocean City, Maryland where I spent a week at the beach with Sara and her family. I had a wonderful time. We had good weather and while the water could not be compared to beaches in Jamaica, it was nice to have a change in scenery.

About my productions, Sorrel was my best piece, and you are right, no one here can pronounce that word correctly. For all the productions, I was both the producer—writer of the materials, and the director of the productions in the studio. The talk show was a little wild. No, I didn't write the script for the actor/actresses. I gave them the topic and they took it in whichever direction they chose. My job was to watch the monitors in the control room and anticipate where the action was taking place in order to make camera switches and to direct my crew members.

While I am in Washington, I will visit the embassies to find out what should be done about visas. My friend Goretti, from Zambia, told me that she doesn't think I need visas for any of the African countries because I am Jamaican, and Jamaica belongs to the Commonwealth like the African countries. I will inquire when I go to Washington.

About graduate school, I still plan to attend. I know about putting together a portfolio. I will do that for Washington. These are my three choices for graduate school: American University, University of South Carolina and either University of Miami or University of Florida. I plan to take the GRE's in October. This semester I will go through the application process because the Spring Semester will be a rough one. I wish there were someone here at E-town who could advise me on all the Graduate School stuff with visas and questions like that. I figured that American U is a big school, so maybe someone there can give me some insights.

My semester in Washington will give me 15 credits for my internship and seminar class as well as my elective course. I won't need to take any extra courses in my final semester because I took the maximum number of courses through-out my Freshman through Junior years. Things are going o.k. I am slowly packing up my stuff for Washington. I have enough clothes, shoes, and accessories. I know you will miss Jay when he leaves, but somehow you always manage to cope. I haven't heard from American U concerning finances. I figured when I get the bills, I will contact Jim for a check as you suggested. Take care and write soon.

Love Always
Sidoney

On August 27, 1996, I started my senior year at American University in Washington, D.C., which was vastly different from

Elizabethtown College. It is a major university in the heart of the nation's capital. The campus was huge. Elizabethtown could sit in one tiny portion of the campus. Initially, I felt like a freshman all over again, trying to maneuver a new campus with a new roommate in a new city. All the participants in the Washington Semester Program were hosted in the same dorms. This was beneficial as we all tried to figure things out together. In addition, we took many of our core courses together with students from all over the country participating in the program, and we all took our electives with other American University students not participating in the program. It was a unique program, and I was learning from the best and brightest in colleges and universities all over the country.

Being in Washington D.C. during an election year was exciting because I was seeing up close how the U.S. government worked. I had the opportunity to visit the White House, and my group met with Newt Gingrich, who, at that time, was the Speaker of the United States House of Representatives. I was also excited to see how the press corps worked. I joined other college students and volunteered for Bill Clinton's campaign for U.S. presidency. We got mailers together, answered telephones, and ran errands. I was never interested in politics before arriving in Washington, D.C. There, you can't get away from it. I remember the night we learned that Bill Clinton won the election. Meeting him was the highlight for all the interns.

I had other memorable highlights. I took African Dancing for one of my electives. It was hard to believe that I was receiving college credits for dancing and having a good time. The instructor was an eclectic Black woman from West Africa. She taught us the art of using our bodies, especially to the beats of the drums. I liked the challenge of learning something new, and the dance was accompanied by the history of the West African culture.

My internship as a reporter brought me to Capitol Hill, where I had to listen to numerous hearings that affected the wellbeing of children. I would return to the newspaper where I was interning to draft my stories. This was my first "real" job in my major, outside of a college setting. I was learning but in a different way. My lessons were not all in a classroom. The bulk of the lectures that made up the program in the Journalism School was to challenge our thinking and push us out of our comfort zones and make the correlation between politics and journalism. I was also learning so much about myself during this time in my life. Perhaps because I didn't have many classes that required several exams for the first time in my higher education career, I had time to relax. At first, it was hard to figure out what to do with my new-found freedom. I had choices: I could curl up with a book or I could explore a new city with friends whom I made in the program. I decided to explore. I went to museums, bars, did some shopping, and even enjoyed a few lectures on the American University campus. In fact, I found myself going out most weekends.

I'm very goal-oriented, and personal life always took the back burner until I met my West African boyfriend in 1996 while I was in Washington, D.C. Let's call him "Amir." I was young and looking forward to a new relationship. I remember when we had our orientation for the Washington Semester Program and we were warned to be careful of interactions we had. I was careful; in fact, I had my friends accompany me on the first date and they stayed close by in the event anything went wrong. I didn't date much during college. At this point in my life, I was close to achieving my dream of obtaining my degree, I was doing well in my internship, but I threw caution to the wind and began dating Amir. He was nine years older than I, and I wasn't sure where the relationship would go once I returned to Pennsylvania. I was young and in love. I enjoyed exploring the city with a significant other. It was different for me—the attention from someone of the opposite sex, the late-night calls, the intimacy—one would say, all part of maturing. I realized I didn't have to achieve my dreams at the expense of not living and exploring where a relationship would take me. I was scared because it was something new, but I was also excited because it was something new. Despite my initial reservation, I had fun in D.C.

November 2, 1996

I met a really nice guy who is hard working. The way we met was interesting. I was on my way to The White House, and I was waiting by the metro stop for two of my classmates who were getting bagels from the shop across the street. I was there for about 10 minutes when my classmates beckon to me to meet them at the end of the escalator. I was on my way down the escalator when I heard someone calling me. I answered, but I wasn't sure what the guy wanted. He asked me to wait at the end of the escalator. He caught up with me and he said, "I saw you standing up there, and I thought you look so beautiful that I had to come up to you." At first, I was puzzled, perplexed, and anxious to get away because I was running late for my appointment. I finally agreed to give him my number, and as they say, the rest is history.

I never forgot my number-one purpose of being in Washington D.C., to get an education. I had decided to apply to graduate school, and being at a large university, I could get some of my questions answered in terms of how the application process would work from an immigration perspective. I met with the counselor for the international students and learned that in order to attend another university, that school would apply for my student visa and I could then continue my education. Armed with clarity on the path forward, I prepared my applications. I applied to the graduate programs in the schools of journalism at American University, the University of South

Carolina, the University of North Carolina Chapel Hill, the University of Florida, and Miami University. This time around, I didn't need Aunt Bev to help me, like she did while I was in high school. Elizabethtown College had a rigorous journalism program that prepared me to handle advanced studies. My graduate school applications included recommendations from professors, as well as samples from my internships in both journalism and public relations and work for the school newspaper. I submitted my applications, and I waited.

Handling disappointment was all part of the growing up process. I had the grades, stellar recommendations, and the experience in the media and public relations to get into graduate school, but why did I receive a rejection letter from American University? I was angry and disappointed. After all, I was at American University taking classes with some of the same professors who would be teaching my courses in the graduate department. The rejection letter did not say much. It basically said, "While you have an outstanding academic career, you are not a good fit with our graduate school." I was waiting on the response from three other schools, and I feared this would also be their response. For the first time since starting this journey in the pursuit of higher education, I was scared. I feared failure. I was afraid that my journey would come to an end, and I feared that I would let myself down. I decided to get more information. I made an appointment and met with the Dean of the Graduate School of Journalism at American University.

The graduate program at American University was a one-year master's degree program. The dean was very frank with me. He explained that due to the intense nature of their program, they do not accept students directly from an undergraduate program. Their preference was to accept students who have worked in the field of journalism for a few years because they could contribute more and do better in the program. I received the same feedback from the University of North Carolina Chapel Hill, saying I lacked professional experience. While I was disappointed, I realized that everything happened for a reason. I also wondered if I really wanted to remain in D.C. due to this new relationship I was pursuing. I knew that God doesn't make mistakes, so I patiently waited for where He wanted me to be. I didn't have to wait long. Soon, my acceptances came from the other schools, and I decided to attend the University of South Carolina (USC). I made all the necessary preparations to attend USC. A master's degree would be different from an undergraduate degree. The bulk of my courses would be in the School of Journalism, and I would take some elective classes in the School of Business.

December 4, 1996

I can't believe it, but I am now 22 years old as of this day. It's amazing how this year flew by. I went to my office party and then Amir took me out to dinner. We went to a Jamaican restaurant in Adams Morgan for dinner. I had a good time. Amir is so sweet, I hope this lasts. We are both so different. He is much quieter than I am. I am determined to learn his language. How hard can learning French be? I'm kidding myself; it's going to be hard, but I am willing to try so that's all that matters.

My relationship with Amir was blossoming. As the date drew near for me to return to Pennsylvania, I began to wonder how I would manage a relationship with both of us living in different states. I had no idea how we would make a relationship work long distance, but there were feelings stirring up in me that I didn't even realize were left dormant from some time ago. I had reservations. How will this continue? I lived in Pennsylvania, he was in the Washington D.C. area, and I was planning to go away to graduate school in the fall. It crossed my mind to just enjoy myself while it lasted and then go back to my real world once I returned to my college campus in Pennsylvania. Each reservation was met with a plausible solution. He could drive to Pennsylvania at least once a month so we could be together. I could spend all my breaks with him. *People have successful long-distance relationships all the time,* I thought. I began to see the possibilities, and that is exactly what I did—I began a long-distance relationship: late-night phone calls into the wee hours of the morning, trips to Washington D.C., and a vacation to Florida for spring break.

At the end of December 1996, I returned to Elizabethtown to finish my last semester of college. I rented an apartment off campus within walking distance since I didn't have a car. At first, it felt a little strange being back on such a small non-diverse campus. I missed the hustle and bustle of D.C. I also missed Amir and the time I became accustomed to spending with him. I didn't have too much time to sit around and reflect since I was at the final lap to get my first degree. My last semester was filled with completing all my necessary coursework in order to walk across that stage in May. Senior Seminar was, by far, the most difficult course and one that many seniors dreaded. I didn't; in fact, I embraced the challenge. I did my research, put my project together, and confidently made my presentation.

I found that a long-distance relationship was difficult with a hectic school load and Amir's job demands. We relied on daily phone calls to keep the relationship going. Amir visited once a month, and we were together on all the school breaks.

Graduation from Elizabethtown College was an epic moment for me. It's hard for me to explain. I never knew this day would finally come. You might be wondering why. When you want something for so long, sometimes when it happens it seems surreal. All the important people in my life were there to witness me walking across the stage. Mom came from Jamaica. This graduation had a special meaning for her. She had to let her only daughter go in pursuit of a better life. She was my support system from afar. Mom brought Carey with her while Dwayne had to stay behind in Jamaica because of his school schedule. Godmom came from Botswana, and she too was my support system from afar. Aunt Bev and Uncle Jim, other extended family members and friends, including Amir, who were all my local support system, were in attendance. When my name was called and I went up to receive my diploma, I enjoyed hearing the applause and screams from my family and friends. I knew I couldn't have done it without all their support.

May 18, 1997

Graduation is finally here! I can't believe that I have made it so far. If someone told me five years ago that I would receive a BA degree I wouldn't have believed it. It was a beautiful day spent with all my loved ones. My Mom and Carey were there as well as Godmom. Of course, my sweetheart was there looking handsome as ever. He got the chance to meet the whole family. I did it! This is just the first stage for me; the master's is next. Look out world, here I come.

After graduation, we had a party at Jim and Doris' house (Jim is Godmom's younger brother). Jim and Doris helped me a lot while I was in college. I always knew that if I was ever in a difficult situation, they were just a phone call away. This graduation celebration had another special meaning. I introduced Amir to my family and close friends. For many of them, it was the first time I had introduced a man I was dating. I was nervous because I wanted their approval. Amir's charm, smooth talk, and infectious smile won over everyone. I spent the time interacting with my village that got me over the finish line. I was finally a college graduate. I could not have done it without the encouragement and strength I received from my mom, the belief and push that I got from Godmom who saw things in me that I didn't believe were possible, and the support I had from Aunt Bev and Uncle Jim.

I was even calmer as I faced my next challenge: attending graduate school. I knew that Elizabethtown College had prepared me to take on the challenges of graduate work. I was looking forward to the challenge for the next two years while I pursued a master's degree. I spent a month in Washington, D.C., hanging out with Amir and getting to know him better, and he introduced me to his family and friends. I was dating and just relaxing before starting the next chapter in my academic career.

August 8, 1997

Amir and I made it safely to Columbia. Thank God, what a long journey. Thank God for sending me such a loving and caring man. He drove me all the way to Pennsylvania to pick up my stuff then ten more hours to Columbia. We had a good trip. I learned a lot more things about Amir. Our relationship is blossoming, and I hope to God that we can survive the distance between us. Amir and I talked about our dreams and desires for our relationship. I reached my new apartment, and moving in was quick and swift. Thanks to Amir's manpower, everything was in by the twinkling of an eye. Amir also helped me unpack, and boy was I happy about that. He stayed with me for three days to get me settled. We drove around, went grocery shopping, and even took a walk to where my classes will be held. After spending a month in D.C., Amir and I became so much closer. It is going to make saying goodbye even more difficult. I am not looking forward to it.

I arrived in Columbia to attend the University of South Carolina. I was in a new city, and immediately I fell in love with the weather, which was different from the frigid temperatures in Pennsylvania. My apartment was centrally located so that I could easily get to my classes. The university was huge compared to Elizabethtown. I knew no one in South Carolina, but this was no different than when I first arrived at Elizabethtown College. I had an apartment all by myself, but a lot of the residents in my building were also students at the university.

August 21, 1997

The first day of classes. I am both anxious and scared. I know that I can do whatever I put my mind to with God's help. This is no different. I met a new friend Pushba. She is from India, and she is also in the master's program for journalism. She lives across the hall and luckily; we are in three classes together, so now I will have someone to walk back from classes with. I was a little nervous because my classes end at around 10 p.m., but now I am more relaxed. I had my toughest course today, statistics. The professor seemed nice and all, but I know that I will have to work my butt off in this class. I'm not entirely too worried because I am used to hard work...

I did not like living in South Carolina and had a difficult time adjusting to life in the south. I believe it was a combination of several factors that contributed to my state of mind. Being in a long-distance relationship was hard, and so was not knowing anyone. Graduate school was not like undergraduate school; most classes were at night, and the students were older. I also noted the relationship between Black and White people was different. For the first time since leaving Jamaica, I was home-sick and depressed. It was hard to shake off. Race relations in the U.S. was a very puzzling phenomenon for someone who was not raised here from birth. As a child growing up in Jamaica, I knew I was Black; however, that was not amplified until I migrated to the U.S. During my early days in the country,

I was stunned at how much focus was placed on someone's skin color. Everywhere I went, people told me that I was Black. From my observation, race was such a polarizing issue. Lancaster was diverse, and yet it was not diverse. Being with my Caucasian host family meant that I was usually the only Black face in the room. At church, social gatherings, or even at the mall, people stared and made inappropriate comments at times. While my high school was diverse (54 percent minority), where I lived was not. South Carolina, at that time, appeared segregated to me. Although segregation was supposedly a thing of the past, where I lived was very much segregated. The minorities lived and interacted on one side of the town, and Caucasians on the other.

Being in South Carolina brought race relations to the forefront of my mind, simply because of how different it was there. If truth be told, when I was looking at graduate schools, race relations did not cross my mind. I hated the frigid winters in Pennsylvania, so at the top of my list was a warmer climate. I did not like the rural atmosphere, so I wanted to be in a larger city. While I was in South Carolina, I observed that Blacks and Whites did no co-mingle. It was different for those of us attending the university because we were from all over the country. For locals, however, it was a different story. I noticed that not only did Black and Whites not interact regularly with each other, but when they did, something occurred that I never observed while I was in Pennsylvania or Washington, D.C. Black people did not look White people in the eye when they were interacting. There was a sense of uneasiness that I had never observed in myself before either. I was more alert and paid attention to my environment.

When my apartment lease was up, I found a roommate and moved to a two-bedroom house. I was looking for a roommate, and I didn't care about the individual's race. My roommate was a Caucasian woman from New York, whom I got along well with. However, we quickly learned that when we were out in the community, we were an anomaly. A simple thing as going to the grocery store had race implications. When we went to the grocery stores in the "Black" neighborhood, the meat and produce were of a lower quality, to the point that some of the vegetables did not look edible. By contrast, when we went to the grocery store in the "White" neighborhood, we had the best meat and produce, but we had to put up with the constant stares. Also, when we split up, I had to deal with the store workers following me around, I guess for fear that a Black person couldn't possibly afford to pay and would steal. I was uncomfortable in South Carolina, and I felt like I was on a different planet. I put all my energies into my studies and my job. My plan was to finish my degree and get out of South Carolina as quickly as I could. While I was adjusting to a new environment, managing a full-time graduate course workload, and an assistantship, I had no idea that a storm was on the horizon.

Living in South Carolina meant that Amir and I saw little of each other. Being in a long-distance relationship where we went months without seeing each other was exceedingly difficult. I did not adjust well to South Carolina. I started feeling depressed all the time. I did not have a support system, and that made it even more difficult. Every chance I got, mostly on breaks, I went to Maryland to visit Amir.

September 20, 1997

I went to visit Amir. I just got too overwhelmed with not being able to cope with everything. I had to get out of this backwards, lonesome place. Being with Amir gave me a sense of contentment. I could relax without thinking too much about all my problems—possibly failing statistics, being lonely and not making the graduate school connection just to name a few. Being with Amir these few days taught me that I really don't have much to worry about. He continues to show me how much he cares just by his warm touch and comforting words. I had a good visit. I have been working so hard on my body, but I don't think Amir noticed. I am down to a size 9–10. I guess I am happy about it, but I wished he would have commented. I am finally making the connection and putting my life together. A size 8 doesn't seem too hard to reach now.

The first semester of graduate school was my hardest. Despite the challenges of being away from everyone I knew, and being in a new city that I didn't care for, I persevered and finished the semester with decent grades. I pride myself in not letting challenges interfere with the goals I set out for myself. Ever since I left Jamaica, Christmas has always been the one holiday that I struggled with because of how deeply I missed my family and the "traditional" Jamaican Christmas during that time. Since I didn't have my Jamaican family here in the states, I spent the holidays with Amir and his family.

December 25, 1997

The air is filled with happiness, merriment, and joy. Amir and I got up around 9 a.m. and I had a long day ahead of me. We will be hosting six people over for dinner and as host, I will be preparing the main course. I did rice and beans and roasted chicken. Amir's older sister came over and did the fish for us. I am so happy that Amir loved his presents. The coupon book was a hit. He really liked the idea of his woman offering him treats. He got me a beautiful coat and a nice outfit. He is really good with picking out nice clothes. I called home and my Mom and family seemed o.k. and were enjoying their holiday. I was so nervous, I really didn't think I could have pulled it off, but I did. I miss my family this Christmas, but I can say that this Christmas is one that is memorable. I was surrounded by loved ones and friends and that made all the difference. Everyone seemed to enjoy the meal, and we talked, danced, and took pictures. I am so happy that I have Amir in my life. He really made this Christmas one that I will not forget. He showed me that love comes in all directions. There are many things that I have to thank God for—good food, wonderful friends, loved ones, and a caring and wonderful man in my life.

My second semester in graduate school was much better than the first. I had adjusted to the environment in South Carolina, and I met a new girlfriend, Shika, who is also from the Caribbean, so we shared a similar cultural background. I was focused more than ever in my course work because I had a new goal, which was to finish my graduate course work a semester early so that I could leave South Carolina and do my practicum in the Washington D.C. area. It was a great plan that required me to focus on managing my courses with my work schedule of teaching computer graphics to undergraduates in the Journalism School. I had a new focus and goal, and I found that I was no longer feeling as depressed as I did during my first semester. I spent the summer of 1998 working as a reporter at a local newspaper in Maryland. I was receiving practical experience in the area of journalism, which was the career I planned to pursue once I graduated with my master's degree. I enjoyed pitching story ideas to the editor, interviewing the subjects for my stories, and putting the work into crafting the best stories that represented my subjects. My greatest accomplishment was pitching and getting acceptance from the editor for me to have my own column in the newspaper. I enjoyed my summer, and it was great because Amir and I got the chance to be with each other. While everything was going great with my career and my relationship, I began having unexplained abdominal pains. What started in January 1998 as occasional abdominal pains intensified over the summer. I had a mysterious illness that had doctors puzzled.

It's hard to believe that I have neglected you for eight months. So many things have happened. I'm in my final semester of my graduate career and I'm determined to see it through. Of course, I have fears. Will I pass Comps? Will I get a practicum that pays? Will my health hold out for the entire semester? For the past three months, I have been having abdominal pains. I've been to numerous doctors, conducted hordes of tests and they still don't know what's wrong with me. Despite the medications, the pains are still coming. I'm fearful and scared, but I can't let it take over my life. I'm taking matters in my own hands. I'm going to start taking my vitamins and exercise regularly. I guess it can't hurt. Beginning tomorrow, I'm turning over a new leaf. Maybe it will help these pains go away.

Life Lessons From This Chapter:

- Come out of your comfort zone and try new things.

- Hard work pays off.

- Life is also about living—work hard and play hard.

- Dream big—the sky is the limit.

- Education is the key to an immigrant's success.

CHAPTER 3

SETBACKS—THEY CAN MAKE OR BREAK YOU

"If you can't fly then run, if you can't run then walk, if you can't walk then crawl, but whatever you do you have to keep moving forward."

—Martin Luther King Jr.

Who knew that my darkest days were ahead? I had it all figured out, I was well on my way to getting my master's degree, and then my life turned upside down. It's amazing how situations can change someone's life course. I have always been a planner, setting goals and always striving to accomplish them. I pride myself in my ability to plan how I want my life to go, but you know what? Sometimes life never goes the way we want it to, and we encounter a curveball. It's how we handle that setback that builds character. The career path that I wanted to pursue after graduate school was journalism. I had dreams of being successful in the media, with a goal of being an on-air anchor at one of the affiliates in a major media market. I was well on my way. Then one day, an illness changed everything.

At 23 years old, I had accomplished one goal and was close to completing another. I had my bachelor's degree and was in my final semester of a master's degree program when something happened that stopped me in my tracks. I was young, energetic, and full of life. At 5 feet 4 inches tall, I weighed 135 pounds, working out an average of four times per week to keep in optimal shape. I was healthy and had no health concerns, but a series of abdominal pains changed my life. When the pain started in January 1998, I went to the doctor in search of relief. Even though the doctor did not know what was wrong with me, I didn't panic because the prescription he gave me took the pain away, although temporarily. I was better...or so I thought. Three months later, the pain came back in full force. This time, I realized that whatever I had was no joking matter as the pain became debilitating. At first, I thought, *Oh, the pain will go away in a week like it did before*, but this time I was wrong because the pain only intensified. I started seeing multiple doctors, trying to figure out what was wrong with me.

First, I was diagnosed with having an ulcer. After taking medications for that diagnosis for weeks with no apparent relief, I knew that was not the problem. The next diagnosis was a stomach virus, and the antibiotics that I was prescribed seemed to work for a while, but then the pain came back. The next one was irritable bowel syndrome, but the prescribed medication did not work, just as the previous attempts failed to provide relief. I was getting tired of all the x-rays, CAT scans, intrusive tests, and probing that the doctors were doing, without any apparent results. While all this was going on, "Ms. Pain" never left my side. I couldn't drive, I couldn't eat, and I was just not myself. Despite this setback, I tried to keep up with my classes because I was determined to graduate on time.

One of my worst episodes occurred when I was at home studying, and I started having sharp abdominal pains. I tried to ignore them as best as I could. The pain continued until I was doubled over. I really couldn't take it anymore, and it was not relenting.

I ended up in the emergency room. I felt all alone and in pain. I was worried about my courses, and I felt like giving up. What was the point? I didn't know whether I would get through this episode. I picked up the phone and I called Godmom, in tears. At the time, she just happened to be in Washington, D.C., for work. Godmom, who hates doctors and hospitals, got on a plane and came to South Carolina and spent three days with me while I was in the hospital. I was a pitiful patient; I whined, I cried, and I was miserable. Despite my illness, life had to go on. As an immigrant, it was my responsibility to keep up to date with issues concerning my status in the country. The university was hosting an information session for international students who were considering working in the United States after graduation. I put Godmom to work and sent her to the session so that she could gather the information for me. There was not much else she could do but hold my hand while I endured the sharp pains. Just having her by my side throughout the ordeal was comforting, however. Fortunately, after a week of prodding and probing, the doctors had a diagnosis.

I was diagnosed with Crohn's disease on September 18, 1998. After nine months of unexplained chronic abdominal pains, numerous medical tests, frustrations, and fears, I had a name to put to this "mysterious" illness. Since I was in my final semester of graduate school, handling a chronic disease was an unwelcome imposition. My only consolation from the week-long hospitalization was finally having a name to explain all that was happening to me.

Crohn's disease is a chronic digestive disorder that causes inflammation in the lower part of the small intestines, called the ileum, but it can affect any part of the digestive tract, from the mouth to the anus. It can be difficult to diagnose because its symptoms are similar to other medical conditions. The disease affects males and females equally and seems to run in some families. Doctors say that about 20 percent of people with Crohn's disease have a blood relative with some form of inflammatory bowel disease. Carey, my older brother, had similar experiences with his bowels. I have a strong feeling that he, too, had Crohn's disease's but they could not diagnose it in Jamaica.

Although many theories exist about what causes the disease, unfortunately, none of them have been proven and the medical community has no clue as to the exact cause. The most popular theory is that the body's immune system reacts to a virus or a bacterium by causing ongoing inflammation in the intestine. The doctors explained that I would have the disease for the rest of my life and that I would always be on medication in order to manage it. The most troublesome news that I received was that there was no cure for Crohn's disease. I couldn't believe it. I was astounded that with all the advances in medicine, there was no cure for this illness. I really thought that only HIV was in that category. This news was overwhelming for a 23-year-old to handle, who before this diagnosis had no major health problems. The fighter instinct in me kicked in, and I was determined to find a way to live with this disease without allowing it to take over my life.

September 20, 1998

Thank God for yet another day. I guess the severity and seriousness of this disease hasn't hit me yet. At 23, it is hard for me to imagine that I will have an incurable disease for the rest of my life. What does that mean? Am I going to be taking 14 tablets a day for the rest of my life? All I know is that right now I have to live one day at a time. Today, I feel just a little bit stronger. The dizziness is not so bad today as it was yesterday. I'm still having trouble sleeping at night, the cold/hot spells keep happening, but I hope with time my body will adjust...It's amazing how we take little things like health for granted. I know that from now on I won't take anything for granted. Another day I've made it, thank God.

September 24, 1998

With each passing day, I learn something about this disease. Yesterday was not one of my good days. I had great plans and intentions. I planned to go to my two classes and to attend my group meeting. This did not occur because "Pain" paid me a visit. I did everything. I took the medications, I drank a lot of liquid, but nothing seems to help. Basically, I just gave up the fight and resorted to laying on the sofa all day. I can't help but worry about how many more days like this one I will have. I guess I still have to give my body time. It has been through a lot in a short amount of time, and it needs time to adjust. Despite the pain, I can feel my strength slowly returning to me. Each day I feel just a little bit better. The dizziness is still here, but it's not as frequent as it was before.

I was having a difficult time handling my disease with no support system around. I felt like giving up and forgetting about everything I was trying to pursue, especially on those tough days when the disease flared up. Amir and I spoke several times a day. He tried to comfort and encourage me from afar. The phone calls worked for a while, but it wasn't enough. Eventually, he came to South Carolina for a visit.

September 30, 1998

A lot has happened in the past couple of days. Amir came down on Thursday to be with me. I was so happy when I got back from class, and he was there. With this disease being unpredictable, I'm just living day-to-day. On Friday we had a good day. Amir drove me to my internship. I received my story assignment, then we stopped at the J-School so that I could

introduce Amir to Shika (my girlfriend). We went grocery shop-
ping, got my cell phone hooked up, and even went to the gym
where I tried doing a little aerobics. This sort of accomplish-
ment was just wonderful for me. I felt like I was back to my
old self. Saturday, however, was not a good day. I was having
a little pain in the morning, but that later escalated. Amir and
I had such an episode, and he got upset and he told me that
he doesn't think it's a good idea for me to move in with him in
December. At first, I didn't handle the situation well because
I just got up and stormed away and made myself busy. After
Amir got out of the shower, we started talking about it, and
a lot of things were running through my head. I swore that
Amir was just using my temper as a mask for the real reason
why he didn't want us moving in together. I just felt that may-
be he couldn't handle my illness, and a commitment to move
in together was just too much. Amir got upset; he got dressed,
packed the van, and was ready to drive back to Maryland.
At this point, I thought I had lost my baby, and I started crying,
hysterically. The doctors are right, stress doesn't work well
with this disease. As I cried, the pain became more intense,
intolerable to the point of being unbearable. I guess the whole
episode scared Amir because he was right there beside me
helping me. The rest of Amir's stay went well. He's so good to
me, I can't ask for anything more. He cooked for me, cleaned
for me, drove me around, rubbed my stomach and held my
hand when the pain intensified.

In the beginning, it was difficult to handle the symptoms that
accompanied the disease. I had to learn how to slow down.
That was not something I was accustomed to doing since I was
always on the go. In addition to my graduate school course
load, I taught step aerobics at the gym and served as a teaching assistant for computer graphics to undergraduates in the
School of Journalism. This disease turned my life upside down.
At that time, I was a vegetarian, and the doctors explained that

this way of eating was not best for my disease because the fiber from vegetables was contributing to my flareups and that there were some nutrients that my body needed that I could only get from meat. I was paired with a nutritionist from the hospital who helped me incorporate meat back into my diet.

November 9, 1998

I can't wait to be off these stupid steroids. My emotions are in a state of havoc with constant mood swings. To top it off, I'm getting fat again and I feel like there is nothing I can do about it. I just can't seem to stop eating. The more I eat, the hungrier I get. It wouldn't be too bad if I were doing constant aerobics exercise, but when the pain is here, I just can't work out. I can't seem to win either way. I stepped on the scale and topped it at 145 lbs. It just depresses me. I know how difficult it is to lose weight. All the weight is going into making my stomach bigger, and my love handles have enlarged. Maybe I'm overreacting, but I don't know if I could deal with myself if I got fat again. I worked so hard to look the way I do. Going from a size 18 to a size 10 is a great accomplishment, and I don't want to go back to where I was. I just want my old life back, but this Crohn's disease is screwing up my entire life.

Have you ever had a carefully laid-out plan and then something happened that caused you to rethink the way you were going? I began to question everything, especially whether the career path that I had chosen would be conducive to a chronic illness like Crohn's disease. As part of my master's program, I had to get a practicum, which is basically an internship in my field of study. I secured a practicum in the public relations department at Special Olympics International. Before my diagnosis, I had plans of doing my practicum at a television station or at a newspaper, but my disease changed everything.

Miraculously in December 1998, I successfully completed all the coursework for my master's program. I moved to Maryland where Amir and I began living together. This was my first time living with a man, where I had to share bills and make compromises. There were similarities, in that we were both immigrants, but there were major cultural differences. In May 1999, I completed my practicum, passed my comprehensive exam, and completed all requirements for my master's program. I had a choice to make: I could either go back to South Carolina to participate in the graduation ceremony or I could have the school mail my degree. I did not want to go back there, so I had them send me the degree in the mail. What was important for me was the fact that I persevered. Despite the medical setback, I completed my advanced degree on time.

Journalism is a career field with high stress, and I quickly learned that stress is a major trigger for the disease that I now had to live with for the rest of my life. I was becoming skeptical of pursuing a career in journalism. My first major life choice after being diagnosed was to alter my career path. I gave up my dream of being in the media and, instead, entered Corporate America in the field of public relations. I secured my first job in a small company, doing corporate communications.

Life Lessons From This Chapter:

- A chronic illness doesn't have to be a death sentence.

- Managing stress is key to survival with a chronic illness.

- Learning how to pivot when things don't go as planned is crucial.

- A setback is an opportunity for a comeback.

- Never give up.

Chapter 4

I'VE GOT THIS?

*"Be careful for nothing; but in everything by
prayer and supplication with thanksgiving let
your requests be made known unto God."*

—Philippians 4:6 (KJV)

E very woman wants to have it all: a wonderful job as
well as a spectacular personal life. While it might look
different for each of us, that's a goal that many of us
strive for. What does it mean to have it all? That answer will
differ from one woman to the next. For me, it meant being
married, having children, and having a career where I was
respected and rewarded for my contributions. When I entered
Corporate America in 1999, I felt like I was on cloud nine and
was well on my way to conquering the communications field.
As a young woman in my mid-20s, I was also looking forward
to taking my relationship to the next level, toward marriage
and starting a family. I was keen on building my professional
and personal life.

I started my career as a Communications Associate at a government contracting firm in Rockville, Maryland, a 10-minute drive
from my house. I was excited to be in the workforce. I had many
internships, but this was finally a full-time role in the communi-

cations field. The small company was owned by a husband-and-wife team, and I was happy in the interview when they said they were open to the H-1B visa process. I was so excited to land this position that I didn't bother to ask all the right questions at my interview. After a six-week search and countless interviews, I was just happy that I found a company that was willing to pay me what I was looking for and to sponsor me for immigration purposes. I was excited that I got the opportunity to work in the U.S., and I was ready to put my degrees to good use.

The communications department consisted of my boss and me. I learned quickly that the advantage of being in a small company was that I had a chance to wear many hats. As someone new in my career, I was eager for the opportunities to learn and show what I could do. My first big assignment was to create an internal newsletter for employees and an external one for customers. As a government consulting company, many of our employees were in government buildings in Washington, D.C., with a small segment in the headquarters' office where I worked. I conducted telephone interviews with those employees and interviewed the ones who were in headquarters before putting a plan together on the content, frequency, and reach of the internal newsletter. For the customer newsletter, I interviewed the owners and some of our clients for input. I was proud of the outcome of my first major deliverable.

One of our vice presidents was an African American woman who took me under her wings. She was responsible for bringing revenue (government contracts) into the organization. She saw my eagerness to learn and imparted some of her knowledge to me. I will never forget one of our conversations. She explained to me that as a Black woman, I will always have to work twice as hard as my Caucasian colleagues to advance in my career. At 24 years old, I had no clue what she was talking about. I was happy that I had a job and figured

I'm accustomed to hard work, so that shouldn't be a problem for me. Later in my career, I would more fully understand the knowledge she was trying to impart.

Some Americans take it for granted that they can get a job wherever they want, and if things don't go well, they can just change jobs and go to another company. For many immigrants, changing jobs is not a simple process. In fact, in many instances, immigrants have to stay in jobs where they are not treated well—either they are being paid less than their colleagues despite similar qualifications, or they are not given much-deserved promotions and have to stay because their visa is tied to that company.

I spent eight months at this company before I began looking for a new job. I realized that their business model was not as sound as I thought. The company had one major government contract, and when that contract was not renewed by the government, the financial viability of the company came into question. Some of the senior leaders began to leave. When my boss left, I knew I needed to find something quickly. As a non-citizen, I couldn't just go out and get a job like any American could. As an international student, once I finished my degree, the U.S. government gave me the opportunity to be employed in the United States for one year. My challenge was that as a foreigner, I had restrictions associated with my work permit. In short, I was only allowed to legally work in the United States for a company that agreed to sponsor an H1B visa for me once my one-year work permit expired.

I began searching for a new job because I did not want to be caught in a situation where I was out of work and not compliant with my immigration status. I made a vow to myself that I would stay away from small businesses and I would pay attention to the financial viability of any firm that I'd plan to work for. My manager found employment at a consulting firm, and she knew I was looking for a new job and so referred me for a position in their D.C. office in the Communications Department. I made it through a few rounds of interviews. I was hired at a consulting firm in Washington, D.C., and the best part about this role was that I was making an additional $8,000 on my annual salary.

December 4, 1999

I can't believe that I have reached a quarter of a century. How the years fly by. I guess the 25th birthday is an important one. I'm mid-way between my 20s and 30s. I think this is a good time to evaluate my life so far and my accomplishments or lack of accomplishments. I think for my age, where I am coming from and all the adversities that I have had in my life, I have done well for myself. Materially, I have a nice car, a beautiful home, and a good job that can help me provide the basic necessities in my life. While these are all good, materialistic things are not the only things that one should value when judging accomplishments. I think I have accomplished a lot by finishing my bachelor's and master's degrees before my 25th birthday. Despite my Crohn's illness, I persevered and obtained my master's. Most importantly, I have people in my life who care about me and love me. My mom and brothers are always there for me and love me for just who I am. Godmom is another person who has been there for me. I can always count on her when I need her. Sometimes, I believe I don't deserve all that she does for me. God is good, and He is always looking out for me. Last, but certainly not least I have a wonderful man in my life. He takes care of me; what more can a woman ask for? I think something that I wished that I would have accomplished by now is a more spiritual presence in my life. Deep down, I want to get God back in my life in a big way. I wished that by my 25th I would have my weight in check, but because of recent health setbacks, I will have to get motivated to accomplish that goal. Something else that I had hoped to accomplish by now is more permanence in my relationship. Things are going great with us, but by now I had hoped that we would be engaged. I'm hoping that that is on the horizon. I know that we will spend the rest of our lives together. I guess I'm just ready to be a Mrs. I have faith that it will come in time. For my 25 years, I have done so much, seen so much, and have so much more to experience in life. My Sweetie was so great because he catered to my every need, and he took me out to dinner. Thank you, God, for allowing me to live to see 25 years. I hope that I will live to see many more. I was a little depressed to turn 25, but this could be the beginning of great things to come. I believe in new beginnings, and this is surely the right time for that.

When I started my job at the consulting firm, my main concern was to ensure that I was doing well to produce work for my clients, that I remained active on my government contracts, and that my bosses on my various projects were pleased with my results. I was working on communications projects for various government agencies, including the Environmental Protection Agency and the U.S. Department of Housing and Urban Development. When I started at the new company, I had four months left on my work permit, so they started the process of applying for an H-1B visa for me. The H-1B is a non-immigrant visa that allows U.S. companies to employ graduate-level workers in specialty occupations that require theoretical or technical expertise in specialized fields, such as IT, finance, science, etc. I had a lawyer who was handling the case. Every immigrant will tell you that immigration lawyers are not all created equal. In addition, immigration laws change so frequently that immigrants can only hope that their lawyer is on top of things. I have heard of countless cases over the years of lawyers preying on immigrants. There is fear in the immigrant community: fear of not knowing the system, fear of retribution if abuses are reported, and fear of being deported back to their home country.

When I started the petition process with the Immigration and Naturalization Service (INS) for my H-1B visa, I constantly asked my lawyer about what would happen with my job if the INS did not approve my petition before my current work permit expired. Her response to me was always the same: "You will be fine." Call it intuition, but I had a gut feeling that something was not right with her answer. I was four days away from my work permit expiring when she informed me that I could not work until the INS approved my H-1B visa. I had to give my job a two-day notice that I couldn't return to work. I ended up taking a thirty-day unpaid leave of absence from my job. One minute I was doing a job I absolutely loved, and the next minute I was transferring my workload to someone else.

May 11, 2000

I went into the office today, and I was greeted by many of my coworkers who wanted to know if I was back for good. That made me feel good to know that my fellow employees think that I am valuable. My lawyer would barely give me five minutes of her time to discuss this new INS development. She said she hasn't received the INS request as yet and she will let me know. It's a shame, but I don't trust this woman who is supposed to be representing me and have my best interest at heart. The whole situation with the INS and my lawyer has left me depressed. I felt like crap all day. I just wanted to find a hole and crawl in and never come out. How did things get so bad? I know that I need to snap out of this funk, but I can't, and it didn't help that I didn't work out today.

I was nervous and scared because I had a mortgage, car note, car insurance, and other bills. That was probably one of the toughest thirty days of my life, while I waited on the INS. My early experience with immigration and originally being denied a visa made me worry. Fortunately, after one month, my H-1B visa was approved, and I returned to work, where I was placed on a project of a lifetime. I was working on an Energy Star® program in California, doing press conferences and promotions on Energy Star® appliances. I had an opportunity to stay in California for one month, splitting my time between San Francisco and Los Angeles. In the words of Walter Jolley, "A setback is just a setup for a comeback." Throughout my ordeal, I trusted God to guide me every step of the way. My career was back on track, so what could go wrong?

I quickly learned that as a Black woman, they did not teach me in undergraduate or graduate school how to deal with inequalities in the workplace. I was all alone in figuring things out. Being in Corporate America is not a bed of roses, especially for women of color, and I discovered this while navigating my career and the inequalities I was experiencing. I foolishly thought that talent, hard work, and stellar performance were the criteria that led to advancement in a company. Throughout my career in different industries and different companies with different bosses, the bottom line was the same. There are two different types of criteria, one for Caucasians and another for minorities.

I experienced many inequalities in the workplace. These situations were exceedingly difficult for me to handle, especially since I had it in my head that the solution for career advancement was to get educated and excel, which I did. I entered the workforce with rose-colored glasses. I had the knowledge, the right can-do attitude, and I pushed myself to work above and beyond. Despite all these traits and successes, moving up in my career was at a snail's pace and, in some instances, never materialized.

I observed colleagues with less experience, who contributed less to the businesses, and who had questionable work ethics, pass me by leaps and bounds. It hurt because the deciding factor was something I couldn't change. When I entered a room, I couldn't leave my "Blackness" at the doorway. They say women should ask for what they want. Whoever invented that phrase does not know the plight of women of color. You can ask until you are blue in the face, and you can outperform year after year, but the reality is that this group, especially African American (Black) and Latina women, lags behind other races in terms of compensation in many companies around the country. We talk with each other and we share our experiences, but unfortunately, they are the same for many of us, whatever the industries, titles, or companies. When things go wrong, we are the first ones to be blamed. When performance ratings are given out, we usually receive the lower ratings. Working under these circumstances can take its toll.

Being in the workforce for more than 20 years, I've experienced my share of inequalities. I will share the two most memorable examples. This is to help someone realize that you're not alone if you're experiencing something similar. As difficult as your situation might be, you can overcome. I did it!

I was a middle manager with direct reports at a company where I had been working for four years. The environment in the department had become toxic, and I began exploring other career possibilities. I made the decision to move to a different area in the organization. At my last team meeting in my old department, my manager had a catered lunch as a goodbye celebration. During the meeting which consisted of six employees—my manager, my two direct reports, and my two peers— one of my peers made an inappropriate comment: "Sidoney, I am going to bring you a roll of tissues because you are going to need it to wipe (the leader I was supporting)'s a$$." While

I was disappointed with her statement, I wasn't surprised because this woman could say whatever she wanted, and she got away with it because our boss said nothing. My response to her inappropriate attack was "Nothing you throw my way today is going to upset me." The next thing that happened should have never occurred, especially in the workplace. Our manager, who was a Caucasian woman, took a piece of garlic bread and threw it across the room and hit me on the side of my face, and almost everyone laughed at my expense. I was flabbergasted, and my response was "Oh, my God, you just hit me with that bread." Someone made a comment that my boss got me, to which she responded that she was on the basketball team in high school and she still had it in her to get the target. I was the only Black person in that room.

I was in shock because I couldn't believe this was happening to me in the workplace. I was humiliated, especially because my direct reports were also in the room to witness what had happened. I got up from the meeting and walked back to my office to think. I didn't want to have a knee-jerk reaction. I remained at work for the rest of the day, and my manager never came to me to apologize. I shared what happened to me with people who were in my personal and professional network to get ideas on how I should address this unfortunate situation. I knew I had to do something, but I had a lot at stake. At the time, I was a single mom trying to rebuild my life, so it was critical that I made the right decision so that this incident did not negatively impact me. One of the things I considered was to seek legal action because this was an assault in the workplace, and if the roles were reversed, I would have been immediately escorted off the premises for doing something like that to my direct report. I felt that I had to do something so that this manager would not do something like this again to any employee, and especially not to another Black employee. I decided to file a complaint with human resources (HR). This incident happened on a Friday, so before I left the office, I scheduled a meeting to talk to the HR business partner on Monday morning.

Ladies, I wish I could tell you that reporting my manager to HR had a positive outcome. This was White privilege at its finest. I explained everything that happened to me in detail. I provided the names of the employees who witnessed the event and described how I felt when the incident occurred. My HR business partner told me that an investigation would take place to find out what happened, the head of the department would be informed, and she would get back to me. I asked her if I could discuss the situation with my manager, and she agreed.

I worked for that manager for a year and a half, and during that time, I had to deal with her passive-aggressive tendencies towards me. However, hitting me in the face was crossing the line, and I wanted to confront her about her behavior. Later that day after I reported the incident, I went to my manager's office. What transpired between us was really sad, and the worst part was that I believe this individual was not sorry for what she did to me. I believe she was just trying to cover her tracks. She essentially told me that I told her to hit me. Of all the ridiculous things that could have come out of her mouth, that one showed that she was scrambling. When I denied giving her permission to hit me, she changed her story and told me that someone on the team told her to do it. She later gave me a half-apology and said, "You know I was joking, right? If I offended you, I'm sorry." I told her I did not find the incident funny and that it did hurt me.

My organization did not protect me after I reported that horrific situation. I left that department a few days after that, hoping to put the incident behind me and move on to my new department. It was a difficult situation, but I was determined not to let it stop me from doing my best work and progressing in the organization. This incident occurred right before Thanksgiving, and I was on vacation that week. I returned to the office to my new normal, and it was not pretty.

At that time in my career, I was naïve about White privilege, office politics, and the power of influence. My ex-boss decided to retaliate against me, and she got away with it. Not only did she get away with it, but she also terrorized me for eight years while at the company. Since she was more senior than I was, she had more influence with the senior leader whom I was supporting in my new role, and she did her own spin to the leader. By the time I returned from vacation and started my new role, that leader told me that she was cautious about me working for her because no one likes an employee who runs to HR. I again explained what had happened to me, but she told me I should have given my ex-boss an opportunity to fix things instead of reporting her to HR. This was a bummer because my fresh start in my new role was now complicated and stained.

The next hit came during my review, which was done by my ex-boss and delivered by my new manager. The entire review was filled with lies. I had my mid-year review with my ex-boss in September (this should have occurred in July, but she was not a timely person). I received glowing feedback, all my deliverables were in line with my goals, and there were no problem areas identified. I left the department at the end of November, and the reviews were done in December. They retaliated against me for reporting something that happened to me. I received one of my worst reviews from my ex-boss. I will leave you to draw your own conclusions.

Enduring the attacks, the passive-aggressive and sometimes aggressive behavior from this ex-boss, who was two levels above me, was not easy. I had several managers during this time, and no one would help me, simply because my ex-boss had more influence with the senior leaders in the company. Other leaders who witnessed her behaviors towards me would say something to me in private about how unfortunate the situation was, but no one stood up for me. Due to her influence, no one wanted to confront her and risk rocking the boat. This is the opposite of courageous leadership. What could I do, go to HR again? That was out of the question because I believe that it would have only made the situation worse. Ladies, you might be wondering why I didn't leave. I stayed because I was a single mom with three mouths to feed and therefore, didn't have the luxury of walking away from a good-paying job.

What was my coping strategy? I worked hard and ensured that my work was top shelf. If I wanted to stay around, I had to make sure that it would be difficult for her to convince leadership to get rid of me because I was excelling in my projects. Despite my stellar work, I never advanced because of her influence with senior management. This was unfair, but believe me when I tell you this happens in Corporate America all over this country more often than it should. While what happened to me was unfortunate, I learned how to fight, and to fight hard! I became more resilient, and I grew in my career by taking on stretch projects and proving my worth. That, ladies, was something that my ex-boss could do nothing about. I am not the first Black woman to suffer through an unthinkable situation at work while those in positions of power looked the other way and allowed the abuses to continue.

My second example happened at a time in my career when not much shocked me anymore, but this one still stands out. I had a client for whom I worked tremendously hard. As a public relations person, raising the profile of my clients was one of my main goals, and it was one I could influence. I had spoken numerous times with my manager about my prospect of getting promoted, and I received one frivolous answer after another. There were never any concrete areas of improvement identified nor direction of what I needed to change in order to make that career jump. I received feedback, such as, "You need to have executive presence" and "You need to be seen as strategic and not tactical." I took these very vague responses and devised a plan that I believed would get me the promotion I was seeking.

This strategy required a multi-year plan. I worked the plan, and I was able to get my client a coveted prestigious external award that would be a highlight of any public relations career. As a result of what I was able to do for my client, I too received two very prestigious company awards. I was on cloud nine when I sat down with my boss to get my annual performance review. I was confident this would be the year I would be promoted to the next level. Boy, was I wrong. I was blindsided, and I received one of the lower-than-expected performance ratings that stated I "met" expectations. This essentially equated to an average performance. I was speechless because I couldn't believe what I was hearing. I pressed my manager and brought up my recent accomplishments that happened within the review cycle, and he said my support of my client was inadequate. How could that be when I received numerous internal and external awards for the work that I did? Welcome to the life of women of color in Corporate America. I have had numerous episodes in my career where I couldn't see the light at the end of the tunnel and the stress of the inequalities affected me more than I wanted it to.

December 17, 2001

I woke up this morning and I really did not want to get out of bed because I knew what was awaiting me at the job. Today was an exceptionally long day, and I have a splitting head-ache as I write this entry in my journal. I'm not being treated fairly at work, and it is tough to keep my head above water.

I finally found a project that will provide professional growth, and my boss is giving me a tough time and not willing to allow me to pursue it. For the first time in my professional career, I stood up for myself. I had to let my boss know how I felt. The discussion went on and on in circles for hours. At the end of the day, I was pretty much wiped out, and to top it off, I still have an unbelievable amount of work to do. I don't know how this will turn out, but I have to take my professional career in my own hands...Regardless of how this turns out, at the end of the day, I want to be able to say I did the best that I could.

July 1, 2002

A part of me feels like just giving up. I have prayed to the Lord numerous times to help with my job situation, and now I feel stuck with no way of getting out of this place so I might as well just keep my mouth shut and just take whatever these people are dishing out. I guess that is how life is. When you don't have choices, you just have to endure the inequalities and try to find coping mechanisms. As I go into work today, I need something to lift my spirits. Something to make me want to stay in the building. Unfortunately, I don't know what that something is. I get paid less than some colleagues, even though I am more qualified. I get treated like a child, and I receive no respect. My work is constantly used by others, for which I receive no credit. I could go on and on. For me, I guess my only hope is trusting that God will make a way out of no way.

For the past two decades that I've been in the workforce, diversity and inclusion have been buzz words in Corporate America. I've never felt truly included at any of the places I've worked. I was constantly judged, not by what I bring to the table but by the color of my skin. Interest in someone like me takes on a different spin. I had companies invest in my professional development, but it looks and feels different. From my experience, when I entered these organizations, there was initially a desire to evaluate my work on its merit. Praises and promotions were within reach during a reasonable amount of time. After an initial bump, then it always became predictable, and my career stagnated. Promotions were few or far between or more often non-existent, and I was encouraged to move sideways, take on stretch projects in addition to my day job, and urged to attend training sessions to "fix" my gap areas. In my mind, these "opportunities" should have led to more coveted promotions, but the reality is they did not. That's not the case for me and for the many women of color I've interacted with at my places of employment and within my network. Why is it different for us? Why do we have to work twice as hard? Why are we not being promoted to senior management levels?

With all the talk surrounding diversity and inclusion, this should not be my experience. Let me enlighten you: In many companies, diversity and inclusion initiatives are nothing more than a "check-the-box exercise," with little to no strategy behind them. This phenomenon will not change until Corporate America recognizes that diversity and inclusion are part of a business strategy and not something nice to have. As I have matured in my career, it has become easier for me to take a stand for what I believe. I am passionate about diversity and inclusion because I get it. I mentor many women, both women of color and otherwise. I am doing my part to educate the next generation of leaders on recognizing and changing the narrative around diversity and inclusion. My hope is that I can help more junior women avoid some of the mistakes I made earlier in my career. I continue to educate, guide, listen, and support women of color in their quest to cope and grow their careers in Corporate America. I believe in the adage "each one, teach one." I will continue to use my influence to impact change. I have to be part of the solution for change. I continue to look for gaps and make recommendations for ways in which we can help change the experience for women of color in my company. Lucky for me, there is a desire and a willingness to address this issue, and that is the first step in enacting change and moving the needle.

It saddens me that not much has changed for the plight of Black people over the past twenty years. The year 2020 brought a major spotlight on racial injustice and inequalities in the U.S., similar to what occurred during the segregation era. This year is one that will forever be etched into the minds of Black people in America. Living in the United States during what I call the "Awakening of America" was not easy. The senseless death of George Floyd, an African American male, at the hands of a White police officer, while three other officers stood by and did nothing, created an outrage, not just in the United States but around the world. There were peaceful protests, but there was also violence, such as looting, destruction of property, and attacks on peaceful protestors. Watching the awful death of a Black man stirred up something in many Black people in the U.S. We were tired of the police brutality, the racial profiling, and the injustices that seemingly were occurring more frequently with no consequences. It started off with a focus on police brutality, but it expanded beyond that. It now focused on the systemic racism that has occurred across the United States for a seemingly very long time.

The spotlight on the Black Lives Matter movement is not new because it's been around for years. However, the real "awakening" and cultural shift this time around was among White people in the U.S. and around the world. They're now our allies in this fight, and because of them, I hope this might be the right time for us to witness real and sustainable change with regard to racism.

This has been a tough week for Black Americans. We all watched in horror a week ago when a white police officer put his knee on the neck of a handcuffed Black man, George Floyd, for almost nine minutes until he died. Despite pleas from George and the on-lookers, the officer never relented. The Black community is outraged, and despite the pandemic, thousands took to the streets in protest. There was also rioting, looting, and destruction of property. This happened not only in Minneapolis where the incident occurred but all over America from New York, Washington, D.C., Los Angeles, and many places around the world. They arrested and charged the officer who committed the crime as well as the other three officers who stood by and did nothing. As a mom of two Black teenage boys, I'm scared. I'm scared of what society thinks about Black men in this country. Black America is tired of the injustices that we have and continue to endure. It's hard to continue to be judged by the color of our skin. Despite the arrest, people continued to protest—Blacks, whites, Indians, Asians. Everyone is coming together in solidarity. I pray for this country, and I pray for peace. God help us.

Like many Black mothers around the country, I was having more frequent discussions with my sons about race relations in America. From the time my oldest was seven years old, I started talking to my boys about how to conduct themselves if they encountered the police. As they got older, my instructions became more specific—answer politely, be respectful, don't reach for anything—the goal is for them to come home safely to me. When George Floyd was murdered, my youngest said to me, "Mom, that man did everything right, and they still killed him. What are we supposed to do now?" I was stunned by the words of a 13-year-old who was looking to me for answers that I didn't have. As a mom, it broke my heart, and all I could say to him was there are lots of inequalities, but he still had to do what he could to remain alive. That was a tough mom moment.

During the "Awakening of America," while many Caucasian individuals were exclaiming ignorance about the plight of Black people, I understood what was happening all too well because I was one of those Black people who was assaulted, disrespected, and terrorized because of the color of my skin. There was no doubt in my mind about that. I was amazed at how many times I heard individuals proclaimed they were not racist, asserting that White privilege didn't exist, yet they would say that the racial issue was overblown and that they couldn't wait for this nonsense to die down.

Corporate America was not immune to what was happening outside of their organizations. Many corporations quickly put out statements condemning racism, and others voiced their support for Black Lives Matter, the movement that was leading the protests and calling attention to the systemic racism that's prevalent in the United States. As Black people, we are accustomed to the initial outrage after the killing of unarmed Black people. Each time, however, things would die down, and absolutely nothing happened. This time felt different, and Black people across the country remained hopeful that now something would be done to change our plight in society and Corporate America.

Like many women of color, I must figure out ways of coping with inequalities in the workplace. I have to make a living; I have bills to pay, and I must ensure that I have a job that affords me the ability to take care of my family. For me, I refuse to remain quiet, and I choose to do what I can to educate and contribute to change. In addition, I draw on my life experiences, my culture, and my faith to keep me going. I've learned that there are, and there will continue to be, inequalities. There is no getting around that, so I have to accept this reality. Jamaicans are hard workers, and this is part of who I am, so I make the decision to continue to work hard, continue to influence, and do everything in my power to show my value and worth.

The most difficult part is how to handle the snide remarks, the racial undertones, and the discomfort of being judged by the color of my skin. I would be lying if I said this part is easy. How do I handle it? I pray for God's guidance. While dealing with the challenges at work, I also have a life to live, and I had to shift my energies into focusing on my life outside of work. As someone living with a chronic illness, I have plenty to deal with. Focusing on my personal life helped to ease some of the career pressures that I experienced. This was the same strategy in 2020 as it was in 1999 when I began living with Amir.

Living with Amir brought new realities to my world. Compromising was a big challenge for me. Somehow, in order to keep the peace, I was the one who was always giving in. At that time, we had been dating for five years, and we started discussing the possibility of marriage. I was pleased that we were heading in that direction because it bothered me that we were living together and unmarried. I knew the teachings of my faith, and it was difficult for me to fully commit to the Lord with the way I was living. I kept these thoughts to myself and instead invited Amir to join me at church on Sundays. Amir only met Mom and Carey at my graduation, so I invited him to Jamaica for a two-week vacation in order to introduce him to my extended family.

December 18, 2000

This has to be one of the most memorable days of my life. In front of my family as witnesses, Amir asked me to become his wife. Mom, my stepfather George, Carey, and I went to Port Royal in Kingston to have dinner by a seaside restaurant.

Sidoney Samuels-Buckridge **101**

The meal was delicious, and after the meal, Amir wanted to get a shot of all of us with the camcorder. He wanted my stepfather to shoot the video, but I suggested some Americans who were at a table beside us so that my stepfather could be in the shot. Little did I know that the man of my dreams was getting ready to ask me to be his wife. He did it. Amir got down on his knees in the gravel and asked me to marry him. This is one of the happiest days of my life!

I returned to the United States with joy in my heart. I was so happy. As soon as I got home, I got on the telephone to share my good news with all my family and friends. Planning a wedding for the first time was nerve-wracking since there was a lot that went into an event joining two families together. I was my own wedding planner and handled all the logistics. I wanted to ensure that God was part of the equation as I prepared to become a wife. I always attended church on Sundays once Amir and I started living together. I would invite him, and sometimes he came, and sometimes he didn't. I began praying because I wanted him to have a strong relationship with God like I did. I knew that I couldn't force my faith on him, so I got down on my knees and prayed. I prayed that the Lord would save him. To my absolute joy, when we met with the minister to discuss our marriage and receive counseling, Amir decided that he wanted to give his life to God. I was so happy because, I thought, now we could share our faith.

We decided to be celibate while Amir went through his teachings and his baptism preparation. I thought Amir would object because he was new to the faith. To my surprise, he did not. But I must say those six months before our marriage was not the easiest time to be living in the same house, sleeping side-by-side in the same bed, and being celibate. I saw this as an opportunity for me to re-dedicate myself to God and the principles of the Church and to enter into the marriage the right way.

On May 4, 2002, in front of 100 guests representing our family, friends, and colleagues, Amir and I exchanged wedding vows. We promised to be there for each other through the good and the bad times. I was 26 years old, and looking back on that day, everything went well. Mom and Godmom were there for me, along with my extended family. I felt like a princess in a fairy tale and I was marrying my African king. After the wedding, Amir and I spent a week in the British Virgin Islands for our honeymoon. With such a promising start, I went into this marriage with all that I had. I wanted to be a good wife, I wanted to love this man forever, and I wanted him to love and protect me. Who would have thought that someone like me would be so lucky?

Even though we lived together for a year and a half before we got married, there was something oddly different once we walked down that aisle and exchanged our wedding vows. The reality that I was legally responsible for the wellbeing of another person was something that finally hit me. It was no longer just "me," but it was now "we." Right after we got back from our honeymoon, Amir was laid off from his job. Luckily, we went the route of having a wedding that we could afford, so no money was owed to any vendor after the wedding was over. That was truly a blessing because I now had to cover all the bills for the family until Amir got another job. During Amir's three months of unemployment, I was his cheerleader and coach. I helped him write his cover letter, reviewed job postings, and provided tips on negotiating salaries.

Amir was a man accustomed to working, so he struggled during this time. I was a supportive wife, encouraging him until he got back on his feet. I ensured that we were spending time doing things together so that he was not consumed with worrying about his unemployment. We continued to attend church together and remained connected during the week with our faith. We read the Bible and prayed together. For me, this was nothing new, but for my new husband, it took a little getting used to. For so long, I prayed that I would get to a stronger place in my faith. Being married and no longer living in sin, I seized that opportunity. It became easier to talk about my faith with Amir and I didn't have to drag him to church. Now he wanted to go.

I went into the marriage with openness, but what I thought it would be wasn't the reality. Early on, I began to notice some things about Amir that I wasn't pleased with, such as not wanting us to take vacations, forgetting my birthday, and concerns around money. I quickly discovered that now that we were married, everything was centered around money. Amir expressed that spending money on anything other than our bills and his business venture in West Africa was foolish. The phrase "our money" became a constant whenever I wanted to make a purchase or spend money on experiences. I brushed off my concerns and convinced myself that Amir was being cautious because of his recent unemployment. We spent the time enjoying something we both liked doing, working out, which didn't cost money, so there were no arguments around that choice.

Amir was a fitness guru who later became a personal trainer, so helping me push my body to its limit was something we did several times per week. Sometimes, I hated him when the workouts became hard, especially those upper body workouts.

June 6, 2002

I am so proud of myself today. I have been talking about working out, but I just couldn't get my body to just do it, despite the fact that Amir kept waking me up in the mornings. I just couldn't get myself out of the bed. Well, God bless my patient husband. He got me up this morning and even came downstairs to work out with me. I'm so blessed to have the type of husband that I have. He didn't have to get up, and he could have told me that he needed his rest, but he didn't. He also made me some lunch. After my workout and shower, I felt so rejuvenated and ready to take on the day. I missed that feeling and I am going to continue with this lifestyle. My husband even commented that I was smiling more this morning. It wasn't my most powerful workout, but I did my 30 minutes and that was not bad for someone who was on a workout sabbatical for the last month.

Working out was especially important to get my body in optimum shape because, after eight months of marriage, Amir and I wanted to have a baby. With a chronic illness, I had no idea what that meant for my chances of having children. Having a chronic disease made me cautious, and as such, I wanted to get my hands on everything that was out there on Crohn's disease and pregnancy. To my surprise, my research did not produce much information. I turned to my gastroenterologist for help. He gave me a pamphlet and the Crohn's and Colitis Foundation's website as a resource. My gastroenterologist also informed me that based on his experience with women living with the disease while pregnant, they either had flareups throughout the pregnancy or the disease went into "remission" where they experienced no Crohn's symptoms.

Information about Crohn's disease and pregnancy was almost non-existent. I couldn't find much literature out there, so I turned to the Internet. All I found from the medical community were recommendations that women contemplating pregnancy should do so while the disease is in remission. I was so excited to get started with expanding our family. While I was excited, I was also a little nervous because I wasn't sure what pregnancy would mean for someone with Crohn's disease. For the first few years after being diagnosed, I had what is described as moderate Crohn's disease. For the most part, my medication kept my disease in remission. I had flareups on average about four times per year, and in those instances, I was treated with steroids to help manage it. On average, I would end up in the emergency room about twice per year, when the pain became too unbearable and the maintenance therapy was inadequate. I became accustomed to this routine, and I was managing the disease well. While I was nervous not knowing what would happen if I got pregnant, Amir and I wanted a family, and so we pursued it. I was at a healthy weight, and I had no other medical concerns, so I was optimistic and hopeful that I would fall into the group of women who experienced a "remission" during pregnancy. After two early miscarriages, I became pregnant again in January 2004, and that was when my struggles with the disease escalated.

I found out that I was pregnant on February 4, 2004. I was happy, excited, and afraid, all at the same time. I was happy because I wanted to experience the joys of motherhood. Because the disease was active at the time of conception, I feared the unknown. Since October 2003, my disease had been in a severe state. My body was rejecting treatment, and it became increasingly difficult for me to do the simplicities of life—doing my hair, taking care of my home, and working. By January 2004, after an incident where I was curled up in fetal position on the floor in my office, my doctor signed the papers for me to go out on short-term disability. It became increasingly clear that I could not handle going to work every day.

February 4, 2004

I'm pregnant! Gosh, I'm so happy at this moment. I'm glad that my suspicions are correct. The pregnancy test shows a bright red line. I'm so nervous to be happy because of my two previous miscarriages. You know what, I can't worry about that. I just have to have faith that everything will be fine with this pregnancy. Now that I'm home on disability, I'm a lot more relaxed and calmer. My stress-reduction therapy is really a bonus. I hope that I get another month of disability that way, I can stay home, relax, and rest and hopefully everything will go o.k. I called my ob-gyn, and she is going to take blood to test my progesterone and human chorionic gonadotropin (HCG) levels, (HCG is a hormone secreted during pregnancy) *then they will decide whether I should come in earlier or wait for my February 19th appointment.*

This pregnancy was an emotionally difficult time for me. I was not prepared for everything that happened. In fact, it was emotionally draining because I developed complications right at the beginning, and they continued throughout the entire pregnancy. How I handled stress was crucial to getting through the rough spots. The support from family and friends helped me focus on the light at the end of the tunnel.

Being from another country meant that I did not have the support of an extended family close by. Most people were supporting me from afar. I thought I hit the jackpot when I got married, but it turned out that my "Mr. Wonderful" was not so wonderful after all. He did not provide the support that I needed. I felt like I was going through the difficulties of pregnancy all on my own. He was unavailable. I drove myself to the hospital for checkups and doctor's appointments, I remained in the hospital on numerous occasions without many visits from him, and I handled the emotional turmoil by myself. Being alone in another country without a support system was difficult.

As a newly married couple, I thought adding to our family and going through each planning stage would be something that we would be both excited about. Well, I must have watched too many Lifetime movies, because in all those movies, the man was right by the side of the wife from conception to birth. That was not my experience. I felt like I was carrying the burden all by myself and that my husband was noticeably absent at critical points during my pregnancy. If there were challenges and setbacks, I had to figure them out on my own.

When I took a turn for the worse during my first trimester, and the doctors were not sure if I would make it, Mom came from Jamaica and stayed with me for two months. It was a godsend to have her visit the hospital daily, hold my hand during bouts of strong pain, and just listen to my hopes and fears. Being there with me during those two months meant the world to me. At that time, she owned a small variety store, so it was a sacrifice for her to leave her life and business behind to help me out. Godmom was also a pillar of strength and support. While she lived far away in Florida, her constant phone calls offering support or just providing a listening ear provided a source of comfort to me as well.

The difficulties of Crohn's disease are multifaceted. The cookie-cutter approach is not effective because what works for one individual could be useless for another person with the disease. Similarly, people with Crohn's disease have varying symptoms. In a nutshell, no two Crohn's patients are exactly alike. While there are similarities, on an individual basis, there are definite distinctions.

The most common symptoms of Crohn's disease are abdominal pain, particularly in the lower right area, diarrhea, rectal bleeding, and fever. Loss of appetite and weight loss are also common symptoms. Typically, when I experience flareups (when the disease is active) my symptoms are:

- chronic abdominal pain
- constipation
- blood in stool
- loss of appetite
- fatigue

For the most part, I can handle most of the symptoms associated with the disease except for the chronic abdominal pain. This was the most bothersome and primarily the reason why I would end up in the emergency room. When the pain became debilitating, performing the normalcies of life became impossible. During these episodes, I could not eat solid food, move about, nor take care of myself. There were times when my oral pain medications, Vicodin and Demerol, which helped me manage the pain, ceased to work. In such situations, my only choice was to go to the emergency room so that I could receive pain medication intravenously to bring the pain under control.

When I went to the emergency room on February 10, 2004, I just figured that this would be the same, like any of my previous emergency room visits, where I would receive intravenous pain medication, be observed for a couple of hours, and then be sent home. To my surprise, it wasn't. I learned quickly that everything changes when you are pregnant.

My last hospitalization was in 1998, so I was not prepared to handle this new course of treatment. This was the first of numerous hospitalizations for almost a year. I learned very quickly that I needed to be an active participant in my care. In my opinion, if everything were left up to my medical team, I would not be happy with the outcome. My medical situation was complicated, and I was receiving care from two sets of professionals who did not talk to each other. What I found to be most troublesome was that in many instances, they were not in agreement as to the best course of action for my care. I'm not a doctor, so hearing conflicting advice, especially when I was in a vulnerable state and not knowing what choices to take, became problematic. This left me anxious, scared, and wondering whom I could trust.

The obstetrics and gynecology (ob-gyn) team wanted to limit all x-rays because I was in the critical first trimester, and it was feared that x-rays would cause harm to the baby. On the other hand, the gastroenterology team was more concerned about treating me for Crohn's disease instead of worrying about a baby who was not yet "a person." Despite my expressed desire to protect my child as well as myself, I felt like I was being treated like any other Crohn's patient rather than as a pregnant Crohn's patient.

There were numerous conflicts surrounding my care. For the first two weeks of my hospitalization, I was only receiving treatment to control my pain. During this time, a battle arose between the ob-gyn, gastroenterologist, and the surgeon as to what was the best course of action to take. While the doctors fought, I remained lifeless in the hospital bed, getting considerably worse. It took intervention on my part to turn the tide of my care.

During my month-long hospital stay, I experienced numerous complications, including an intestinal blockage, nutritional complications, and a host of symptoms not related to my disease. The following were some of the complications that I experienced:

- Intestinal blockage
- Infection
- Liver problem
- Elevated white blood count
- Pneumonia
- High blood sugar
- Constipation
- Nutritional deficiencies
- Weight loss

We think we should listen to our doctors because they know what is best for us. They have the medical degrees, so whatever they say must be right. I learned very quickly that if I was going to survive, I needed to trust my own instincts. The first week in the hospital was rough because I was not eating much, and as a result, I lost ten pounds during that time, and this was when my first complication began. Because I was pregnant, my ob-gyn team was not happy and ordered the nurses to ensure that I was eating all the meals provided. After two days, I was not passing stool. The nurses provided many options to get my bowels moving, but nothing worked. I insisted that I didn't want to eat since I wasn't going to the bathroom. The nurses scolded me and informed me that I had to follow the doctor's orders and that I had a baby to think about, so I must eat. As a first-time mom-to-be, I had no idea if what they were saying was correct.

My requests to avoid eating fell on deaf ears, and my worst fear became a reality. My stomach became swollen and was the size of a watermelon, and I began to feel uncomfortable without a bowel movement for days. Only then did the doctors act. They had to put a tube down my throat to extract all the excess waste that was there due to my intestinal blockage. This tube remained in place for an entire week. That was one of the most unpleasant procedures that I had ever experienced in my life. I wish I could say that my husband was right by my side during this ordeal, but that would be a lie.

This was my first lesson in patient advocacy. Ladies, make sure that you are an active participant in your medical care. Speak up, ask questions, and don't take the doctors' words as gospel. If something doesn't feel right, go with your gut.

February 23, 2004

I am making good progress, the doctor promised me that the tube would come out of my throat today. That should ease a lot of my discomfort. The pain is almost non-existent, and I'm so glad that I have improved remarkably. The baby is doing o.k. also. This baby is a fighter whom I'm sure will continue to fight until the end. If everything continues to progress, I will be introduced to liquids in a couple of days and if that goes well and I am able to go to the bathroom on my own, I will be released and sent home. I am hoping that I will be able to get out of here by the end of this week. My Mom is scheduled to be here sometime next week to help us out. I put my baby in His hands and pray that He will continue to protect us both.

When I began losing weight rapidly, I discussed my concerns with the doctors about my fear for the baby's life. Since I had the intestinal blockage, it was evident that I could not eat solid food and that an alternate way of feeding me would have to be explored. Some tiny incisions were made into my arm and I was fitted with a PICC line—a thin, soft, long tube inserted into a vein in my arm. PICC lines are used for long-term intravenous nutrition. Essentially, I was being fed with high calories through the veins. I was happy that my baby was getting the nutrients that were required for growth and development because I was aware of how critical the first trimester was to a baby's development. My joke to my family was that for the first time in my life, I could get fat without putting anything in my mouth.

March 5, 2004

Yesterday was one of the toughest days that I've had since I have been here. The Crohn's I know how to handle, but it appears that I developed an infection from the line that gives me my nutrition. I had a pounding headache all day, fever, shivers. Last night got so bad that the nurse had to change my sheets and robe because they were soaked from perspiration. Today, they are running some tests to figure out exactly what is causing me to feel so bad. I thank God for small mercies. Today, the headache is gone, and I feel a lot better. The physical therapist came and gave me some exercise to strengthen my muscles I'm pretty weak from this whole ordeal. Today, I will take it easy. I'm going to watch a bit of television and relax. I just spoke to my mom, and I am so happy that she is coming to help me out. I'm really going to need her to help me get my strength back. Lord, I know that you have been with me every step of the way. Thanks for your help; thanks for your guidance, and thanks for protecting me and the little one.

I just could not take a break. The PICC line was a great idea because it gave my intestines some much-needed rest. Unfortunately, I had yet another setback. The PICC line became infected, and as a result, the doctors had to remove it. This was not good news because I was back to square one. I could not eat anything by mouth, so the doctors were running out of options. An infection was the last thing I needed. An infection meant that the doctors had to treat me with even more medicines in addition to the ones I was already taking. I did not want this, but what options did I have? The doctors assured me that treating the infection as quickly as possible was the best option for the baby. Too weak to argue, I went along with the recommended course of action.

The doctors removed the infected PICC line from my right arm and put another one into my left arm. Since I was scheduled to be released from the hospital, the PICC line would serve the dual purpose of providing nutrients and administering my medication. I was released from the hospital, only to be readmitted a few days later because the second PICC line also became infected. I wasn't having any luck, and to make matters worse, the infection from the PICC line meant that I had to be treated with more medication.

With no PICC line, I was back to having clear liquids to try and provide the baby with some nutrients until my prognosis got better. Most likely, this would have to be maintained throughout the rest of the pregnancy. While this would be difficult, it was much better than having surgery and jeopardizing my baby's life. While in the hospital before my release, I met with a dietitian several times and we worked on a "liquid" eating plan that would provide the baby with nutrients. Boost and Ensure became staples in my diet.

The gastroenterology team recommended surgery to alleviate the chronic state of my disease. They informed me that without the surgery, there was a possibility that I would die, and if I had the surgery, I would most likely have a miscarriage. I was scared. For many days, I laid in my hospital bed, worried that the doctors' prognosis was inevitable. Despite this news, I refused the surgery. Some people did not understand my decision, but I turned it all over to God. One of the doctors said, "You're young; you can have another baby." That really hurt! I wanted this baby. I had experienced two miscarriages, and I could not go through that again if I had other options.

I am a strong believer that God doesn't make mistakes. Trust me, being in the hospital for so long gave me a lot of time on my hands, and so I prayed and prayed. Refusing the doctors' advice was not something that I did without careful consideration and prayer. I kept asking God to show me a sign that my baby and I would make it. The baby kept getting over every hump—good heartbeat, growing and developing, and passing all the doctor's check boxes. I kept asking God to show me a sign, and every step of the way, He did. That was all the validation I needed. So, I called a meeting with my medical team, and since I could not talk because I had a tube down my throat due to the intestinal blocking, I wrote my questions and responses. My main question to the medical team was whether surgery was my only option. When I got pushback from them, I wrote the pointed question, "Are you saying there

is no other option that can save my life except the surgery?"
Like I suspected, they could not provide a yes to that question.
When they could not tell me yes, I informed them that I wanted
a less invasive treatment option that would give my child an
opportunity to live.

March 3, 2004

*Today I feel so discouraged, so tired, and I feel like maybe
I am a sick person. I'm sure you're probably wondering what
has caused my depressed state of mind. Again, today should
have been my day of rejoicing. I was supposed to be going
home, but last night the doctors decided that my white blood
cells are too high for me to go home. I want to be better when
I go home, but I can't help but feel that the longer they keep
me here the sicker I'm getting. I'm really scared. I'm scared
for myself, and I'm scared for my baby. I spoke to my ob-gyn
today and told them that I want the baby to be checked.
Hopefully, they will grant my wishes. I'm so glad that my Mom
will be here next week to take care of me. I just want to put
my head in her lap and for her to tell me that it's going to be
o.k. Lord, I know that you are watching over both me and
the baby. Please watch over Ms. Nieves (hospital roommate)
too because she really needs you right now. Provide her with
comfort and peace of mind. I took a walk earlier, and maybe
later on today, I will take another walk. I feel somewhat weak.
I didn't sleep well last night, so I suspect that might have
something to do with it.*

My first hospital stay during my pregnancy was the longest.
I was subsequently hospitalized eight other times following
my initial stay. While those stays were much shorter, with
an average stay of one week, it did not make it any easier.
Being prodded and poked daily was not my idea of fun. It was
difficult to handle being in and out of the hospital so frequently

and the effect that disruption had on my life. I had to figure out a way to cope with what was now the realities of my life.

When I was first admitted to the hospital in February 2004, I never dreamed that I would be away from my husband for an entire month. Laying in a hospital bed day in and day out was challenging. To make matters worse, I kept getting new roommates and everyone seemed to be leaving, except me. At times, I felt like giving up. I felt extremely sorry for myself and was wallowing in self-pity. If I was asked the question " Tell me one of the most difficult times in your life?" I would have to say this hospital stay was the longest and most difficult 30 days of my life.

Watching a loved one going through such difficulties was not easy for my family, and even for the nurses. I came to know all of them, and I could see the anguish on their faces whenever I took a turn for the worse. The nurses were all rooting for the baby and me to get well enough so I could go home. The nurses offered words of encouragement, and they provided me with tips on how to deal with the doctors. These good deeds helped to make my stay a bit more tolerable. Unlike with the nurses, dealing with the doctors was challenging.

Being in the hospital for as long as I had been left me exposed to numerous infections. Being surrounded by so many different sick people was not a good thing for me, but since everything is governed by what the insurance company decides, I had no choice but to remain in a semi-private room, which meant that I always had a roommate. With Crohn's disease, some of the medications that are required to make me better weakened my immune system. As a result, it was easy for me to pick up bacteria or virus while in the hospital. In essence, the doctors were not only treating the Crohn's disease but everything else that I picked up along the way. I felt like I was fighting a losing battle. The Crohn's disease I was familiar with, but all the other infections and illnesses just made me feel weaker. I didn't have much left in me to fight, but I kept fighting anyhow because that's who I am as a person. My fighter instincts got me through that difficult month of my life.

April 13, 2004

I'm back in the hospital again. I've been here since Friday of last week. My abdominal pains just got so bad that I just couldn't take it anymore. With painkillers, the pain is under control. Today is the first day that I'm a bit better. The good news is that the baby is doing o.k. I have a feeling the baby is a girl, and I have been talking with her constantly. The doctors want to do a CAT scan. While I don't want to expose the baby to radiation, everyone agrees that the danger to the baby is not as bad now that I am in my second trimester. I've been praying a lot, and I know that the Lord will protect the baby and me. The baby is 14 weeks now. Thank God, the baby is doing o.k. Today I had a dream, and now I feel a lot more comfortable doing the CAT scan. I dreamt that I saw Jay (Godmom's husband who died) and he told me not to worry about the baby because everything was going to be o.k. I feel so much better with his assurances. I'm just hoping to continue to do well so that I can get out of here. If they find anything that needs surgery, then that will be the next step, but we will cross that bridge when we get there.

After my third admission to the hospital, I was beyond frustrated, and I wanted answers, which I was not getting. To make matters worse, the conflicting medical advice created a lot of anguish for me. The medical team convinced me that they needed to perform a CAT scan of the abdomen to see what was going on with me. I was skeptical about the effect this would have on the baby, and I asked numerous questions. I consulted my ob-gyn, and she wrote off on the procedure.

She explained that while there were risks involved to the baby, they weren't extensive, and the procedure would help the gastroenterology team figure out exactly what was wrong with me. Despite my reservation, what choices did I have? I agreed to do the test because I had to trust the opinion of my ob-gyn, hoping that she had my child's best interest at heart.

I prayed on the matter and left it in the Lord's hands because I knew that He would lead me on the right path. It was not an easy decision to make, and I did not have the liberty of time on my hands. I had only one day to give my answer to the medical staff. As expected, the burden to make all decisions rested solely on my shoulders. Amir abdicated his role, left all the decision making to me, and never followed up with the doctors. His role was to stop by the hospital a few days per week when he wasn't too tired after returning from work. I was in a state of turmoil because while I worried about my own health, I also wanted to protect the life that was growing inside of me.

On the day the procedure was scheduled to take place, I was informed that the hospital (radiology department) refused to perform the test due to my pregnancy. Instead, they agreed to do an MRI, which posed less danger to the baby. While I was disappointed that my medical team did not discuss the matter with each other and present me with the best course of action, I knew that God was in control and that everything was working out just the way He wanted it to.

After receiving the news about the radiology department's refusal to perform the CAT scan, even though it was presented to me by my medical team as the way to go, I lost what little faith I had left in my local hospital and its medical team. The only doctor's opinion that I valued was that of my long-time gastroenterologist of five years at that time (who continues to be my doctor today). In extreme medical situations such as these, it is important to have a doctor whom you can trust to make sound decisions. My gastroenterologist saw me at my best and worst, and I trusted his judgment in handling my medical care. Since I knew him the longest and was happy with the care that he provided for me, I was more than thrilled when he worked it out for me to be transferred to Johns Hopkins Hospital.

I was hospitalized three times at my local hospital before I was transferred to Johns Hopkins Hospital in Baltimore, Maryland. When you are hospitalized, the team of doctors working on your care is of vital importance. It is essential that you have a partnership, with a common understanding. If you lack confidence in your medical team, then not only will you worry about your illness, but you will also have the added stress of worrying whether you are receiving the best possible care. After my third hospitalization at my local hospital, the medical staff did not know what else to do for me. I was in the hospital again for the same complaint, so it was obvious that the treatment they were providing was not effective.

My gastroenterologist's opinion was that I would receive the best possible care at Johns Hopkins Hospital. That institution has a reputation for having top-rated gastroenterologists who are well-trained in treating high-risk Crohn's patients. I was pleased to leave my local hospital and was anxious to see if Johns Hopkins could help me with my struggles with the disease. The only drawback to this arrangement was that my long-term gastroenterologist whom I had learned to trust would not be able to treat me anymore. I would be solely in the hands of the Johns Hopkins medical team.

My stays at Johns Hopkins Hospital were much more pleasant than at my local hospital. The biggest difference with my new medical team was that they showed equal concerns not only for me but for my baby as well. At my local hospital, I was rooming with the general population of sick patients due to the hospital's policy that a woman must be in her 20th week of pregnancy before she can stay on the maternity ward. Whereas at Johns Hopkins, once a woman is pregnant, be it four weeks or 20 weeks, she can stay on the maternity ward. This made absolute sense to me because being on the maternity ward meant that both the mother and baby would be cared for simultaneously. This was the first time that I felt my baby and I were receiving appropriate care. I believed the medical team had both our interests at heart. Being away from the general sick population cut down on the possibility of picking up infections, like I did at my local hospital. Also, being allowed to stay in a private room, without roommates, made for better hospital stays.

The professionalism of the medical staff at Johns Hopkins was impressive. I especially liked how the medical staff operated when they were dealing with me. Unlike my local hospital where the approach to care involved the doctors visiting and consulting with me on an individual basis, the Johns Hopkins medical team (ob-gyn and gastroenterology) would enter my room together and listen to my symptoms and complaints. This approach allowed all the doctors involved in my care to hear the same information, giving them an opportunity to work as a team to provide me with the best care. Once the doctors reached a consensus, the leader of the medical team would later inform me of the recommended course of action.

I found this approach to be much more productive and caused the least amount of stress and interruptions to my stay. What did I learn from staying at two different hospitals? Hospitals are businesses, and like any other business, some are better than others. Do your homework and shop around so that when you become ill, you will have already done the legwork, and it will help you make an informed decision as to the place that will provide you with the best possible care. Choosing the right hospital makes a big difference, trust me.

Because Johns Hopkins was more than an hour away from my home, I saw less of Amir during my hospital stays. In fact, in some instances, he was only with me at the hospital when he dropped me off and when he returned to pick me up after I was discharged. I was practically on my own to handle my condition and the medical teams. I kept him updated during our telephone conversations though.

Medicine is a fascinating field. I am first to accept the wonders of what doctors can do today. With technology and their training, doctors can perform surgery on an unborn child as well as provide adequate care to a one-pound premature baby who later goes on to live a normal life. These actions are phenomenal. Doctors are not perfect, and they can make mistakes, misdiagnose, and do not always provide accurate information. For this reason alone, I am a firm believer that gone are the days when patients should take their doctors' word as "gospel."

Doctors are humans with their own individual personalities. With my many hospital stays and involvement with doctors, I'm sure I have come across just about every possible personality. There are some doctors who will hold your hand, answer your questions and be patient with you as you digest the information that they deliver. On the other hand, there are others who do not have good bedside manners. They are abrupt, curt, and do not like to be contradicted. My advice is to not let these doctors intimidate you. As a patient, you have rights. One of them is the right to be treated well. Despite their methods, I do believe the main concern of many doctors is getting an ill patient well.

Throughout my ordeal and struggles with Crohn's disease during my pregnancy, I took an active role in my own care.

This is the reason I believe my baby and I were able to survive and have a positive outcome. Even when I did not have the strength or ability to speak for myself, I used the power of the pen. I communicated my wishes and desires by writing them down and sharing them with my doctors. I believe that it was particularly important for the doctors to see that I would not accept what they said just because they were doctors. I held my doctors accountable—that's what I was paying them for. Medicine is not an exact science because there are several ambiguities with a disease like Crohn's. Since I was aware of this fact, I took the doctor's recommendations with a grain of salt. Don't get me wrong, I am not advocating that you ignore all common sense and discount the advice of your doctors, but do trust your gut and ask questions.

I am here to inform you that patient advocacy is not limited to just doctors and medical professionals. The doctors were not the only ones I had to deal with. I had to work with the insurance company that provided my short-term and long-term disability, and that was a nightmare. What I found to be most difficult while I was on disability was the fact that the insurance company was very reluctant to continue to provide me with benefits despite it being a medical necessity. Initially, I received one month of disability, but after that, it became increasingly difficult to convince the insurance company that I continued to be disabled. At one point, I was in the hospital when my disability benefits ran out and the insurance company did not want to renew. They essentially were trying to intimidate me while I was fighting for my life. My doctors did everything they were asked, and the insurance company kept demanding more. They began a cycle of extending the disability two weeks at a time. It reached the point where dealing with the insurance company was such a hassle that it began to interfere with my getting better due to the undue stress I was experiencing. My gastroenterologist became my advocate, following up with the insurance company to extend my disability, and that was a much-needed relief.

My Pregnancy Journey

First Trimester

Spending most of my first trimester in a hospital was difficult, mainly because of all the unknowns and fears. I was fearful of having a miscarriage, fearful of exposing my unborn child to infections, and I was afraid of what the narcotic medications would do, especially in the critical early stages of development. Most of all, I was fearful of surgery that could take my baby's life. At six weeks, when I heard the baby's strong heartbeat, I was elated and optimistic. That was a sign that a life was growing inside me, and it gave me something to cling to.

While most women worry about nausea, vomiting, and fatigue during their first trimester of pregnancy, I would have been happy if those minor nuisances were all I had to worry about. My intent is not to belittle these symptoms because I know that some women experience severe cases. Yes, I had some of these symptoms, but they were less problematic compared to the complications I experienced with Crohn's disease. When I made it out of my first trimester, it was something worth celebrating because it was the farthest I have gone with a pregnancy.

March 30, 2004

I haven't written for a while because I was re-admitted to the hospital on March 24th. I developed another bacterial infection, two in fact, from my PICC line. This stay was not as bad as my previous stay because I wasn't feeling as bad, and I only stayed there for a week. Luckily, the doctors were able to treat the bacteria infection quickly because it was discovered in its early stages. I'm so happy to be home in my own bed and surrounded by my own things. My pain was also treated and became manageable...Thank you Lord, today is my 12th week of pregnancy, so I have reached a big milestone. I saw the baby at my last sonogram, and I was so excited. From here on out, I'm going to focus on my child and myself and let the other less important matters go.

Highlights of the First Trimester

- Hearing the baby's heartbeat for the first time
- Seeing the baby's sonogram
- Making it out of the first trimester safely

Second Trimester

During the second semester, I found out that I was having a son. I initially wanted a girl, but with all my challenges, I just wanted the Lord to bless me with a healthy baby, regardless of gender. With this new information, my task was to get a name for my son. The naming of children is different in the African culture. Our son would get a French first name and an African middle name, where he would be named after a family member. I left the middle name up to Amir, and I decided on Sebastien for our son's first name.

I was hospitalized twice during my second trimester. Luckily, these one-week stays were considerably shorter than the ones in my first trimester. I was treated for the same condition: chronic abdominal pain due to Crohn's disease. The medical staff at Johns Hopkins told me they had limited medical options without causing harm to the baby. Their approach was to get the Crohn's disease under control when I had severe flareups and monitor me constantly on an out-patient basis.

Yesterday I was released from Johns Hopkins Hospital. It felt good coming home again. I'm feeling better with my Crohn's, but I've been here before. I am optimistic, but as the doctors discussed, I would be in and out of the hospital throughout the rest of the pregnancy. I'm keeping a positive attitude. Today is officially my first day home. I was able to make my ob-gyn appointment for Friday, but I had a bit of trouble with the G.I. appointment. I will try again tomorrow because it is important that I get in to see a doctor next week. Hopefully, it will all work out...So far, I'm not feeling too bad. My complaint is that I have a terrible ache in both my thighs. Hopefully, this ache will go away soon. My girlfriend, Jackie surprised me and visited today. It was so good to see her and her one-year old son Jabari. He has grown so much; it's amazing. It was good to have a friend over. She also brought me the book What to Expect When You're Expecting. Now, I can return the library copy. Lord, thanks for protecting the baby and me.

During my fourth month of pregnancy, I had a difficult time with my Crohn's disease. For weeks, I was in pain daily, relying on Vicodin or Demerol to get me through the day. On the one hand, I tried to limit my intake of these narcotic medications because I didn't want my baby to be born addicted; on the other hand, I knew if I did not take the painkillers and get the flareup under control, I would be right back in the hospital. It was yet again another time of intense anxiety and fear. I had been down this road before, and frankly, I was getting tired of the hospital stays.

My ob-gyn team presented the option of a quad screen test, a simple blood test that screens pregnancies for Down Syndrome, trisomy 18, and neural tube defects. Since I was under 35 years old, this test was optional. However, I had been through so many difficulties throughout the pregnancy, had picked up so many viruses, and had taken so many medications that I thought it was a good idea to find out if there was anything wrong with my baby. The test revealed some abnormality for trisomy 18. The doctors wanted to perform additional testing to make an accurate diagnosis. Of course, this was not the news I wanted to hear. But I was determined to remain strong, no matter what.

May 3, 2004

Unfortunately, my pain seems to be intensifying, especially at nights. Saturday night when we got home from Amir's niece's birthday party, the pain came on extraordinarily strong. Last night I didn't sleep well at all and I ended up taking two pills throughout the night and I took one today. The pain is starting again, so I know I will have to take the painkillers again tonight. I hate the fact that I am taking so many painkillers, but the pain gets so unbearable, I just don't have any other choice. I don't know if this is contributing to my pain, but I'm scared about the amniocentesis that I'm going to do on Thursday of this week. I know that there is a one percent risk to the baby. I know that both of us are covered under the blood of Jesus. The Lord has brought the baby and me through numerous obstacles, so I know the Lord will see us through this test, and He will protect us. My mom called this morning, and we spoke briefly. Tomorrow is our two-year wedding anniversary. We don't have anything special planned. With my feeling so ill, it's a blessing that we are together. Our miracle inside my stomach is reason enough for us to celebrate tomorrow.

How Did I Cope When the Doctor Didn't Have Good News?

Nobody wants to hear that something might be wrong with his or her unborn child. The wait was the most difficult part after I received the unpleasant news from the doctor. I had to wait a week before I was scheduled for further testing with an amniocentesis. Amir was not happy with my continually talking about what would happen if we got negative news about our son. I was scared, and I wanted his support. I wanted to talk about what we would do if something was wrong with our child, but he refused to have that discussion. It was one of the longest and most agonizing weeks of my life. The Lord brought me through numerous obstacles throughout this pregnancy, and I felt like he would do the same for this situation as well, but I was scared.

On the day of my test, I drove the 63 miles alone to face the doctors and to get the answers I needed. I received genetic counseling to explain what the increased risk of trisomy 18 meant to the baby. It was difficult to sit and hear that despite all that I had been through with the pregnancy, the baby might not make it. Being alone to hear this devastating information was tough. The genetic counselor told me that babies with trisomy 18 usually do not live past their second birthday, and because of the severity of their symptoms, termination of the pregnancy is usually recommended. I was devastated by this news. But just because there was an increased risk, in my mind, didn't mean this was definite, so I was determined to trust God to work it all out, and I declined termination. I got upset when the genetic counselor suggested that I needed to consult with my husband before making the decision. In retrospect, I'm sure she was just concerned about my making such a major decision without consulting my spouse; however, she was not aware of my circumstances. On that day, I decided that, no matter what, I was bringing my son into the world.

At the time of my amniocentesis, an additional finding was seen on the sonogram, called dangling choroid plexus. This finding has been associated with viral infections, so my amniotic fluid was sent out for viral studies. At this point, I had an additional factor that I had to worry about. Again, I had to play the waiting game. For two agonizing weeks, I waited to get the results of that test. Luckily, my baby did not have trisomy 18. However, they discovered that I had developed a virus called cytomegalovirus (CMV) earlier in my pregnancy, and it was passed on to the baby. I learned that CMV could have some serious effects on my baby. The doctors went over all the possible symptoms the baby could have as a result of the CMV, ranging from hearing loss, cerebral palsy, to physical and learning disabilities. I was again given the option of termination. This was yet another time that I had to rely on my faith to get me through a difficult situation. I was scared out of my mind. However, at that time, all my experiences with medical professionals gave me the courage to listen to their advice and recommendations but to make the decision that I felt was in the best interest of my child. I refused because I felt that my baby was a gift from God, and no matter what the outcome, it was my responsibility to nurture and cherish that gift. That was what I intended to do. The doctors were not the author and finisher of my faith.

May 14, 2004

I am so happy! I just received the best news and I know that God answers prayers. I just got the results of the amniocentesis and my son is going to be o.k.! He does not have Trisomy 18. He has normal chromosomes. There is still an issue with the CMV, and they will look at my next sonogram to see if he's affected, but God is in control, so I know that I don't have anything to worry about. All the pain that I felt, and the sicknesses will all be worth it, once I hold my son in my arms... At least for today, we have so much to be thankful for.

The doctors performed three separate viral studies on my amniotic fluid. The studies revealed that my son was infected with the CMV virus. What the doctors had to tell me was frightening, but I decided that I was not going to spend the remaining five months of my pregnancy worrying about what could possibly go wrong because stress would land me in a hospital, and boy, was I sick of hospital stays. As scary as the information was, I left it in God's hands because He would work it out. Below is an excerpt that I received from the genetic counselor:

> "All three studies revealed the baby to be infected with a virus called cytomegalovirus. If a fetus is infected, there is a 10–15 percent chance that the baby will be symptomatic (affected). It is possible that your risk is higher than this, given the sonogram findings. Symptomatic babies may present prenatally with ultrasound findings such as hydrocephalus ("water on the brain"), growth retardation, or brain calcifications or at delivery with symptoms, including jaundice, a rash, or an enlarged spleen and liver. Approximately 20 percent of symptomatic babies die, while among the surviving 80 percent, approximately 90 percent develop symptoms of the congenital CMV infection including vision loss, seizures, or mental retardation. The remaining 85–90 percent of infected fetuses are asymptomatic during pregnancy and at the time of delivery. Of the asymptomatic babies, 5–15 percent go on to develop symptoms of congenital CMV infection within the first two years of life including vision loss, hearing loss or mental retardation."

The excerpt above indicated that there was the potential that something could be wrong with my baby. Emotionally, it was a tough pill to swallow because everyone wants his or her baby to be perfect, and I was no different. It was especially hard for me because I couldn't help but feel guilty, that because of a virus I developed due to my hospitalization, there was a potential that my baby could develop one of the symptoms that the doctors highlighted.

How does a mother with a baby growing inside of her, whom she desperately wants to be healthy, cope with such news? Here are some of the things that got me through that difficult time.

Coping Strategies

- My belief in God was the driving force that helped me handle the situation.

- I prayed daily that God would give me the strength to handle all adversities.

- I focused on the positives and refused to dwell on the negatives.

- I focused my energy on preparing physically and mentally for the arrival of my son.

- I celebrated every milestone with the pregnancy.

By my fifth month of pregnancy, changes began to occur with my disease, and I was finally starting to eat like a "normal" person. I made a lot of progress, and my doctors felt that I was at a place where I could reintroduce solid foods into my diet. You would think that after five months of eating nothing solid I would be jumping for joy. I love to eat. Who doesn't? But in my situation, food sometimes brought many unpleasant symptoms. As a result, initially, I was fearful of eating.

I had to be extremely careful about my food choices to avoid a relapse. I started off with a low-residue diet, which is low in fiber, and avoided spicy foods, fried foods, and dairy products. This was the typical diet that many people with active Crohn's disease follow. I was finally able to enjoy being pregnant and feed my baby with a variety of food to aid in his development. The artificial feedings were gone, the liquid diets were also a thing of the past, and I took pleasure in enjoying how far I had come.

No pregnant woman wants to hear "You can't be five months; you seem so small." This statement in several variations became a norm for me. At first, I was taken aback that perfect strangers could be so forthright about something so personal. I became concerned about these comments because I knew that I was not able to get the required calories earlier on in my pregnancy. I brought these concerns to my doctors, and I was assured that the baby was at the right stage of development for his age. This helped me breathe a sigh of relief, but the comments still bothered me.

My new eating freedom allowed me to gain some weight, and for the first time since becoming pregnant, I was gaining weight and not losing. This was what I prayed for because, even though the doctors told me the baby would always get what he needed from my reserve, at the back of my mind I always worried that I was just not providing enough that would aid in his growth and development.

Highlights of the Second Trimester

- Learning that the baby didn't have Trisomy 18
- The ability to eat solid food
- Feeling the baby move for the first time
- Gaining some weight
- Looking pregnant

Third Trimester

The third trimester was one of excitement and anticipation as I got closer to the arrival of my bundle of joy. Medically, I was doing okay and managed to stay out of the hospital, which was a huge plus. I still had to use narcotics occasionally to manage pain, but compared to the first and second trimester, this trimester was by far my best. Since my diagnosis of CMV, I had to have monthly sonograms and testing to ensure that Sebastien was growing properly and that he was not affected by the CMV. At my 32-week checkup, I received the good news that my son was growing properly, and the doctors did not see any evidence that CMV had any effect on the baby.

This was the news that I had been praying for and hoping to receive. This took a lot of pressure off my emotional state, and I spent the last couple of weeks focusing on the upcoming birth of my son. During this trimester, I had the joy of experiencing not just subtle flutters but vigorous kicks from my son.

The third trimester was also filled with numerous projects, such as getting the baby's room ready, attending birthing classes, and enjoying a shower. I had mixed feelings about birthing classes. As someone who hates seeing blood, watching a delivery video was hard. I found the discussion around what to expect, the breathing techniques, and the support that spouses could give to their wives and partners to be immensely helpful. Amir attended the classes with me, but I had to push hard to get him to participate because he thought it was a waste of money. For me, it was worth every penny.

Getting Ready for Baby

Due to the difficulties of this pregnancy, it was not until the third trimester that I finally allowed myself to get excited as we prepared for the new addition to our family. There was the task of turning the guest room into a nursery. Amir handled this task, which involved taking off the carpet and putting in hardwood floors, painting, hanging wallpaper, designing the closet, assembling the crib, and arranging the furniture. Who knew that such a little person could demand so much stuff?

July 27, 2004

Today, I am seven months and a week. Time seems to be flying by so quickly. Soon our little guy will be on his way. We are making all the preparations; now all we have to do is wait until it's time for him to be here. Packages are starting to arrive, so I'm so excited about the upcoming shower that will occur in a few days. I'm feeling a lot more tired now than usual. I think fatigue is settling in as I get into my third trimester. I'm trying to rest as much as I can while I can get it in because I know all that will change once our bundle of joy gets here. Sebastien is a highly active baby. He moves around a lot and makes his presence known.

Shower Me with Gifts

There were so many sad moments throughout my pregnancy that a party was just what I needed. Family and friends came to help me celebrate. I had a great time and was thankful for the generosity of the attendees as well as family and friends who were from out of town and could not make it.

The third trimester was the best time of my pregnancy because this was the only trimester that I was not hospitalized. The doctors were not sure what caused the improvement in my condition. It could probably be attributed to the change in medication or to the fact that my body was now accustomed to another life growing inside. As optimistic as I was, the doctors cautioned that the positive change did not mean that my Crohn's disease was in total remission. The doctors warned that Crohn's disease usually flares up after the birth of a child.

The improvement in my condition was beneficial to both the baby and me in terms of drug therapy. For the first time in my pregnancy, I was not relying on narcotics to get me through the day. I was taking fewer painkillers, until I was going through weeks without taking any at all. For the first time since becoming pregnant, I felt like I was safeguarding my baby from harm. I slowly began to do "normal" everyday activities that I was unable to do for months due to constant pain and the effects I felt from the narcotic medication.

Highlights of the Third Trimester

- Finishing the baby's room
- Attending childbirth classes
- Baby shower
- Baby's vigorous kicking
- No more testing

Tips to Handle the Emotional Aspects of Crohn's Disease and Pregnancy— Friends, Family, and Faith

Friends

I consider myself lucky to have wonderful "sister friends" who provided constant support to me. Jackie provided firsthand parenting information that was priceless, especially when dealing with the doctors and interpreting the information they were relaying about my baby. We were pregnant at the same time, me with my first, Jackie with her second child. She served as a listening ear when my fears took over. She always reminded me that my baby was a gift from God and that I had to trust Him that everything would be okay. Jackie visited me in the hospital and at home, bringing magazines and baby books to help me pass the time.

Shika, who lived in North Carolina, was a tower of strength to me. She called daily and was always available for me. She listened to my fears and shared in my joys and excitement, and her concerns were that of a true friend. I recalled a night during my second trimester when I was in the hospital and having a rough night with the pain. I pressed the call button and asked for my pain medication. There was a shift change and it took half an hour before someone finally came to see what the problem was.

By that time, the pain was so intense that I knew immediate relief could come only from having the medication injected through my IV versus taking it orally. Given that I had been dealing with this for months, I knew what worked. The nurse who came to see me refused to give me the medicine intravenously. I asked her to look at my chart, but she said I had to wait for the doctor, who would be available in another half an hour. I knew I wouldn't make it much longer with the type of pain I was feeling. I knew I needed a diversion, and who did I call? My girl, Shika, was able to divert my attention for the whole hour I had to wait for the doctor to come and allow me to get the medication. Simply listening was all I needed at that time when I was all alone in a hospital room, and my sister-friend was there for me. I was so grateful.

Family

While many well-wishers, friends, and family were too far away to visit, the constant phone calls, flowers, cards, and gifts made me realize that I had a large set of extended family and friends who cared about me. This was a boost to my emotional state. There were times when I felt down, and a simple phone call was able to lift my spirits.

Faith

My faith is a big part of my life. I believe that if not for my faith, I would not have gotten through the difficulties of dealing with the complications of my Crohn's disease during my pregnancy. Handling the negative news about the baby and just getting through all that I did required me to take my faith out of the doctors' hands and put it in the Lord's hands. Through it all, I knew that God was in control, and all I needed to do was "Let Go and Let God!" Don't get me wrong; it was not always easy to do, especially when I was constantly receiving bad news from the doctors. What helped me was to put things in perspective and trust God to make a way where there was none.

February 24, 2004

God is good. I thank the people all over the world who are praying for my recovery. God answers prayers, and I am a living testament to that. The nurses on the floor are all amazed at my progress and my recovery. I thank God for keeping me safe and for protecting both the baby and me. I am happy how well my body feels. I know that I am still on the way to recovery, but so far so good. The difficulties that I experienced throughout the pregnancy was a true test of my faith. It is always easy to say, "Why me Lord?" but instead of those words, I kept say, "Lord give me the strength to get through this." What I asked for was exactly what God provided. He gave me the strength to overcome all adversities. What kept me going was the fact that I believed that my baby was a miracle—a gift from God. As a result, it was easy to focus on the good days and just deal with the bad ones. I saw my relationship with God flourished. Before my illness, my hurried life allowed me to use Sunday Service as my main contact with the Lord. During my illness, I enjoyed having a personal relationship with the Lord. This included reading my Bible, and praying. I felt closer to God, and I just poured my heart out to him. I did not take it lightly what He did for me and my baby.

Tips for Handling the Emotional Aspect

- Rely on the support of family and friends.
- Ask for help.
- Focus on the good days.
- Deal with the bad days.
- Find a higher power to believe in.

A Miracle is Born

On Wednesday, September 15, 2004, after 17 hours of labor, my miracle baby Sebastien was born. I went into labor at 36 weeks at Johns Hopkins Hospital, and that is considered early labor, so I was a bit concerned. Since everything seemed normal, the doctors tried to put my fears at ease. There was really no explanation as to why my son decided to come four weeks early. The joke amongst family and friends was that Sebastien was being "starved" in the womb and he couldn't take it anymore, so he decided to make an early exit.

Labor is called labor for a reason—it was the most difficult workout I have ever had. I was accustomed to pain, which is evident throughout this book; however, giving birth to my son was the worst pain I had ever felt in my entire life. Amir was there holding my hand, but he was not my favorite person at that point in time. Why did I have to endure so much pain, while he just stood there? I was given narcotics for pain as well as an epidural, but they were not effective in totally relieving my pain. I experienced short bouts of relief, but for the most part, labor for me meant pain. Despite my exhaustion, when I heard my son's cry, tears of joy began flowing. It brought joy to my heart because I knew that he was alive and everything would work out. It can all be summed up in John 16:21: "A woman, when she is in labor, has pain because her time [to give birth] has come; but when she has given birth to the child, she no longer remembers the anguish because of her joy that a child has come into the world." (Amplified Bible)

I didn't get to hold my son until approximately 45 minutes after he was born because the doctors had to attend to me. It was agonizing. Even though the doctors told me Sebastien was doing fine, I wanted to see him and get my own confirmation. When I finally held him in my arms, all the agony and pain to bring him into the world just vanished. He was the most beautiful person I had ever laid my eyes on. I was so happy at that moment—it was difficult to find the exact words to explain the emotions I felt.

Sebastien

At birth, Sebastien weighed 4 pounds 12 ounces, and he was 17.5 inches long. On the Apgar score, a test given to newborns soon after birth, Sebastien's score was 9 out of 10, so by all counts everything seemed to be on the right track. After nine difficult months of fighting to bring him into this world, I cuddled him in my arms. It was love at first sight for my new bundle of joy. While in the womb, I talked, read, and sang to him, so I was anxious to get to know him and continue the nurturing.

Due to his early entrance, low birth weight, and my difficult pregnancy, the doctors decided to keep Sebastien in the hospital for a few days after I was discharged. Leaving our child behind was tough. All sorts of thoughts ran through my head. *Will my son feel like I abandoned him if he wakes up and I am not there? Will the nurses ignore his cries and leave him unattended, while we are at home an hour and a half away?* The joy of having a baby is walking out of the hospital with your baby in your arms. I broke down in tears when I realized that I couldn't have my son go home with me. The stitches that I received after delivery were not as painful as the ache I felt in my heart, knowing that Sebastien would spend his first crucial days of life away from me. The only consolation I had was the fact that Sebastien was doing well and passing all the tests the doctors were performing on him. Amir and I did not talk much about what was happening. I was very emotional, and Amir was mostly quiet. I believe he was scared that something would happen to Sebastien.

When we returned to the hospital after Sebastien's first night without us, we were greeted with not-so-good news. Tests revealed that our son was anemic, and the doctors were concerned about the possibility that he had CMV. As a result, he was transferred to the neonatal intensive care unit (NICU). Of course, no new parents want to hear that their child is going to the NICU because that is confirmation that your child has serious medical issues. At least, when he was in the regular nursery, he was only being observed. Without question, this news frightened me. When we visited our baby in the NICU, I prayed he didn't have to stay there long. I was trying to stay positive and find something to hold on to. The good news was that the babies in the NICU were constantly monitored, and if there was something wrong with our child, he was in the right place.

While in the NICU, our baby was hooked up to monitors and had all sorts of tubes everywhere. I was scared. It was difficult to see so many tubes and needles in such a tiny body. Watching a needle being placed in such tiny veins was not something a new mom wanted to witness. I tried to keep my tears in check and to be strong, but my emotions were all over the place. I couldn't help but feel it was my fault that my son was going through such an ordeal. If I hadn't been sick, my baby wouldn't need all this intervention. Fortunately, Sebastien stayed in the NICU for only two days.

On September 21, 2004, seven days after he was born, we brought our son home. The emotions that I felt at that time could be described as a kid at Christmas with all the anticipation of the perfect gift. My perfect gift was in the form of a tiny human being who was tough as nails, just like his mom. He went through so much during his first week of life, and yet he was resilient enough to handle it all. Going home day was indeed a day of celebration.

September 23, 2004

Last night I was truly exhausted. I have been feeling light-headed a lot lately and I'm not sure whether it has to do with the blood that I am losing or the fact that I am just so tired. Sebastien finally went to sleep this morning, and I was able to get some sleep for two hours. It felt heavenly. I took him out for the first time today. He went to his first well-baby doctor's visit. Everything is fine with him so far, so that is really good. I can't stop looking at him and being amazed that I helped make this person. It was all worth it, when I look at my child all the difficulties of this pregnancy with my Crohn's Disease seems like a distant memory. Indeed, I'm truly blessed that God was able to allow me to become the mother of this lovely child.

After delivery I was hoping for yet another miracle: getting my Crohn's disease in remission. I knew this was a long shot, but I kept hoping anyway. The gastroenterologists wanted to give my postpartum body a chance to recover before they began testing to determine what was going on with the disease. After the six-week mark, I began a series of testing. Frankly, I didn't need any test to tell me that the Crohn's disease would just go back to "normal." The pain came back, and that was my indication that I still had an uphill battle on my hands.

After the year I had with the disease, nothing would surprise me, so I had to prepare myself physically and emotionally for what was next. I just wanted my life back, one that didn't include constant chronic pain, narcotics, and doctors as my daily staple. I wanted to be able to enjoy time with my son, handle his childcare needs, and most importantly, I wanted a life where my medical condition was kept under control. While a miracle would have been nice, I began preparing myself to seek out the best quality of life that I could.

Handling Crohn's Disease Postpartum

The postpartum period is one with various emotions, lack of sleep, and the highs and lows of the raging hormones. In addition to all these factors, add handling a chronic medical condition, and it is easy to see how difficult this scenario could be for a postpartum first-time mom. The analysis began with a small bowel series and an abdominal CAT scan with IV contrast. The tests revealed that a portion of my intestines, in the ileum, was severely damaged. This explained the chronic pain I've been experiencing for almost a year.

The test results, while they did not reveal good news, provided me with some relief that because my doctor knew exactly what was going on, she would now be able to do something about it. The wheels were in motion to help put me on the road to recovery. After discussions with my gastroenterologist and surgeon, the recommended course of action was for me to have surgery. Getting the surgery done required some planning because I had a newborn I needed to factor into the equation.

Preparing for Surgery

I had four days to prepare for surgery, and I had a lot to accomplish in that short period of time. As a married woman, you would think that all I had to do was mentally prepare myself for surgery. Unfortunately, with the husband I had, I needed to figure out everything on my own. You would think that Amir would have taken time off work to care for his sick wife and newborn during and after surgery. His decision had nothing to do with finances because I was receiving long-term disability payments. Amir never brought up the option of his staying home and caring for us, and I never brought up the issue. Looking back, I didn't want to fight; I just wanted to get myself prepared for surgery. Looking through current lenses, this was a major red flag but one that I couldn't see at that time. What husband wouldn't step up to support his wife who worked so hard and overcame so many obstacles to bring his son into the world? Why didn't I see that? I didn't because of my naivete and the fact that I was fighting for my life.

Who would care for my son while I was hospitalized? Who would help take care of him after I got out of the hospital? What would happen to my assets if I didn't make it out of surgery? These were the questions that had to be answered relatively quickly. Thanks to Doris, Godmom's sister-in-law, for taking care of my son while I was hospitalized. Surgery is not something to take lightly because anything could go wrong. The surgeon explained the risks associated with the surgery she planned on performing on me. While the risk of dying was relatively low, I now had a son to consider, and I decided to get my financial affairs in order. At that point in my life, I did not have a will, and if anything were to happen to me, I wanted to ensure that my assets were distributed according to my wishes.

With relatively no time to get a will done professionally, I turned to the Internet for sample wills, and I sat down at my computer and put my wishes down on paper. It was not an easy task. It scared me to consider the possibility that I may not be around to see my little boy grow up. The will-writing process took me several hours, and during that time I was sad, angry, scared, and overwhelmed. However, despite the various emotions I felt, I completed the will and had it notarized.

As a rule of thumb, I believe it is important to have a will so that you have a say in what happens to your assets when you are no longer around. It is even more important when you have children and a chronic medical condition. I think a good way to look at wills is to recognize that you are planning and deciding what will happen to you, your loved ones, and your assets, and that you are not leaving that decision up to some-one else who might not know what you want. Many things can go into a will, and my advice is to seek a professional to get this done; however, if you are ever in a bind like I was, seek-ing a sample from a reputable source is a good option.

December 12, 2004

Tomorrow is my surgery, and I am beginning to get anx-ious. I got up real early, and I just couldn't go back to sleep. Yesterday was a very hectic day as I spent the time pre-paring for my departure. I made a schedule for Sebastien, packed his bags, and did his laundry. I don't know what is going to happen tomorrow, I can only leave it in God's hands and pray that He will protect me.

Sidoney Samuels-Buckridge   **143**

My surgery occurred on Monday, December 13, 2004. It was scheduled for 7:45 a.m., and I had to be there two hours earlier to prep. Amir and I left our house at 4 a.m. to get to the hospital on time. I tried to use my drive time to calm my nerves and fears. While surgery is not a cure for Crohn's disease, it would remove the diseased areas of the intestines and could put the disease in remission for several years. The thought of being pain-free was music to my ears, and I held on to that as the fear of surgery consumed me. The surgery, which was performed laparoscopically, took three hours, and it was successful. After the surgery, I was sore, tired, and basically out of it.

I remained in the hospital for five days. This was my eighth hospital stay since the beginning of 2004. I had become a regular and knew what to expect. I was accustomed to the routines of the doctors, the nurses' pet peeves, and the little button by my bedside that was a lifesaver when I needed some help. I was in a lot of pain after the surgery. I guess surgery pain is considered different because with this visit, I had a pump that I hit each time I needed pain medication. This was more convenient than my previous stays where I had to beckon the nurses and be at their mercy when they got around to it.

For the first two days, I was heavily sedated and on pain medication around the clock. Eventually, my condition began to improve, and I was able to make baby steps, such as walking and eating. Of course, with my track record, I was very apprehensive about eating because it was the source of so many of my problems. My motivation was to get out of the hospital as quickly as possible to get home to my son, but the doctors made it clear that I would be going nowhere until I was able to eat and tolerate food. I made gradual progress, and with each passing day, I was able to eat a bit more.

I felt guilty that my son needed me and I was not there. In my head, I knew getting the disease in remission was the best thing that I could do for my son. In my heart, however, I couldn't help but feel guilty that I wasn't there for my baby, especially so early in his life. It was inevitable that I experienced moments of sadness when I had too much time to think. I was hoping this hospital stay would be my last for a very long time.

December 16, 2004

I'm feeling much better today. The doctors are pleased with my progress. I understand that the surgeon took out 20 centimeters of my intestines, that is the portion that was damaged from the Crohn's disease. I'm still a bit tired and weak, but that is to be expected...I started on a regular low residue diet and so far, I have tolerated what I ate. It wasn't much, but at least I didn't throw up or get nauseated. The doctors just did their rounds, and they told me that they will be preparing me to go home. God is, indeed, a wonderful God. He brought me through this surgery successfully. Anything could have gone wrong, but the God I believe in was right there with me every step of the way. I can't wait to go home so that I can be with my son and husband... I'm looking forward to getting my life back. I know the Lord doesn't give us more than we can bear. I'm looking forward to celebrating Jesus' birthday with my family.

Christmas Gift

Going home was just the first step. Needless to say, I was in no position to care for a newborn. With my husband not willing to step up to his responsibilities and with no immediate family close by, it became a real struggle. My girlfriend, Jackie, gave me the best Christmas present. She opened her home to me, and she and her mom cared for my son along with her two small children. Those two weeks made my recovery so much easier. Not many people would have done what my girlfriend did; after all, we were not "family" in the traditional sense. But to me, this was the definition of family. I will forever be grateful for my friend's generosity. Her gift gave me the opportunity to heal a lot faster than I would have if I had tried to care for myself and a newborn. The first two weeks after surgery were crucial for the healing process, and a gift from a good Samaritan made it so much more bearable.

New Year—New Beginning

New Year is a time for new beginnings and what better way to ring in 2005—with a "new" me. At four weeks postoperative, I began to feel like a brand-new person. The pain from the incisions had subsided. I was taken off the low-residue diet and could eat whatever my heart desired. I felt like I was in heaven. It had been so long since I was pain-free and "Crohn's-free" that I marveled at the possibilities of living a normal life. The year 2004 was difficult, to say the least, but despite the hardships, I received the most precious gift—my son, Sebastien.

On January 4, 2005, three weeks after surgery, I returned to Johns Hopkins for a follow-up with the surgeon. I was relieved that all was well. At that time, the only discomfort I experienced was occasional pain at the major incision site. In addition, when I moved a certain way or lifted something heavy, then I would experience a bit of pain. This pain felt completely different from the pain when I had flareups. The surgeon explained that I would have occasional pain as my body repaired itself. Her explanation put my mind at ease.

Following that appointment, my doctor gave me the green lights to return to work. After an entire year of handling medical problems, being out of work, and fearing the future, it was good to hear that I could go back to living a "normal" life, which included going back to work. I adjusted to life as a new mom with a little one dependent on me for his care. I found love in this little person who has my entire face. My miracle was worth fighting for as I saw Sebastien grow up and pass all the milestones that the doctors worried that he would not. When Sebastien was two years old, Amir and I started talking about the possibility of having another baby. Amir was initially concerned about what would happen if a second pregnancy was similar to what I experienced the first time. We did not want Sebastien to be an only child, and despite the struggles I had with my first pregnancy, I was willing to take the risk and try for another child.

Ladies, as you have read about my pregnancy journey, I know you will agree with me that my experience to bring Sebastien into this world could be described as a nightmare. It was a surprise to me when I started yearning for another child. Was I crazy? Was I a glutton for punishment? Again, the doctors had no way of telling me what my experience would be with another pregnancy. I did know that I had to make sure I did not get pregnant while my Crohn's disease was active. I had periodic flareups, but for the most part after the surgery, my disease was manageable with medication. I stepped out on faith and began planning for another addition to our family.

The year 2006 was one of extreme joy and pain. The joy came in the form of a change in my immigration status, and the pain was the loss of a child that I would never see grow up. As an immigrant to the United States, I overcame many challenges to call the United States my home. Many Americans don't have to fight to remain in this country. Like my children, you were born here, and it's a birthright. For me and many others in my situation, we do everything in our power to ensure that we can call the United States home. On February 28, 2006, my dream became a reality: I became a United States citizen. Every immigrant dreams of the day when they can become an American, and I was no different.

My struggles and worries about the immigration process came to an end once I raised my right hand, repeated the words, and heard that I was officially an American during my swearing-in ceremony. I walked away with a nice letter welcoming me as a U.S. citizen.

The White House

Dear Fellow American:

I am pleased to congratulate you on becoming a United States citizen. You are now a part of a great and blessed Nation. I know your family and friends are proud of you on this special day.

Americans are united across the generations by grand and enduring ideals. The grandest of these ideals is an unfolding promise that everyone belongs, that everyone deserves a chance, and that no significant person was ever born. Our country has never been united by blood or birth or soil. We are bound by principles that move us beyond our backgrounds, lift us above our interests, and teach us what it means to be citizens. Every citizen must uphold these principles. And every new citizen, by embracing these ideals, makes our country more, not less, American.

As you begin to participate fully in our democracy, remember that what you do is as important as anything government does. I ask you to serve your new Nation, beginning with your neighbor. I ask you to be citizens building communities of service and a Nation of character. Americans are generous and strong and decent not because we believe in ourselves, but because we hold beliefs beyond ourselves. When this spirit of citizenship is missing, no government program can replace it. When this spirit is present, no wrong can stand against it.

Welcome to the joy, responsibility, and freedom of American citizenship. God bless you, and God bless America.

Sincerely,
George W. Bush

Fifteen years after setting foot on U.S. soil, I now had the rights of every American. As a green card holder, which was what I had before obtaining citizenship, I had more rights than when I was just a visa holder but there were still limitations. The ultimate rights came with the citizenship. I could now vote, serve on a jury, and travel easily to every country around the world. I was on cloud nine. Right after obtaining my citizenship, I found out I was pregnant, so I had two major life events to celebrate.

March 7, 2006

My intuitions were correct. I am pregnant!! My period is late by five days, and I am usually like clockwork, plus I am tired all the time so today at work I went to CVS to buy a pregnancy test and sure enough, it is positive. I got thrown off a bit when I took a pregnancy test last week Wednesday, and it came back negative. I guess I tested too early. I am so happy, yet a bit cautious because of my history with pregnancies, but I am putting it in the Lord's hands. I know that he will take care of me and the life growing inside of me. This news has helped me to put my job situation in perspective. My number one priority is to my family and especially now that I am pregnant, I can't afford to let my job situation stress me out because stress is not good for me or the baby. Lord, thank you.

Suffering a Loss

I was happy that everything was going well with my pregnancy. My Crohn's disease was not flaring up, and I did not experience any pain symptoms. Because I wasn't experiencing any difficulties, I decided I didn't need to return to Johns Hopkins Hospital for my ob-gyn care, and I decided to go with a doctor near my house.

When I was two and a half months pregnant, Sebastien and I went to Jamaica for a two-week vacation. This was Sebastien's first visit to Jamaica and, of course, my family spoiled him. I didn't have to care for my young son, so I was getting a lot of rest. I found that I got exhausted more easily, but that is common during the first trimester, so when I felt tired, I rested. I got back from Jamaica and returned to work as planned. A week after returning from vacation, I had a routine visit with my ob-gyn. I told him about the spotting that I was experiencing, and he assured me that the baby's heartbeat was very strong and that it was not unusual for some women to experience spotting during their pregnancy.

Four days after my doctor's visit, what started as a normal day did not end as planned. During the day at work, I began experiencing a light cramp. After picking up Sebastien from daycare, I got home, and I still wasn't feeling well. I knew it wasn't a good sign when water started gushing down my legs.

Imagine my horror when I went to the emergency room and I couldn't go to the labor and delivery floor, per hospital policy. I had to wait two hours in the emergency room before I was seen. Thankfully, my girlfriend Marie was there with me to try and keep me calm. The most difficult part was that I was 16-weeks along and I had to deliver this little boy whom I had to leave permanently behind in the hospital. Amir arrived at the hospital after I delivered the baby. My heart was broken, and I cried until there were no tears left inside of me. Amir and I got a chance to spend a little time with the baby before they took him away. I was a basket case and was overwhelmed with grief.

I woke up in a sterile hospital with a terrible pain in my throat and in my abdomen and the dull sensation in my heart that a baby is no longer in my stomach. I'm bleeding heavily, I'm in pain, but I would take all the pain in the world if I could have my son back. I never gave him a name last night, and I wish I had because that would make him more real in my mind. I've been asking myself, Why us? And why now? I know that there are no easy answers to these questions, but good God, I want to know why. The doctor gave me until May 24th to return to work, so I might just take all the time.

The doctors say that the pain will go away. I'm sure the physical pain will leave me, but I'm not sure about the emotional pain. I can't stop crying. I can't stop seeing the face of that little boy that is supposed to be mine. That little boy who came into the world way too soon. That little boy who should still be growing and developing in my womb. I know that God knows all things best, but it still hurts. It hurts so much that I can't feel anymore. This is even more difficult because I feel so alone. I feel like I'm going through this difficult process all by myself. Emotionally, Amir is not there for me, physically he's not here either. I know that he has business to attend to, but he hasn't altered his schedule one bit to be there for me. When I asked him what time he was coming home, he acted as if I committed a crime by asking him that question. Is it too much to ask that he comes home and hold me a little tighter for a bit longer? I guess it's too much to ask. I'm feeling so emotionally drained that I know that I'm a basket case. I lost it tonight crying and just couldn't keep it together. I know that God doesn't give us more than we can bear, but right now, I'm not sure I believe that.

I believe my doctor was wrong, and the spotting I experienced four days prior was a sign of the miscarriage. I had gotten past the first trimester, so I didn't think I had anything to worry about. My two previous miscarriages were during the first trimester. It was hard for me to make sense of what was happening to my body. This loss was extremely difficult. I grieved alone and that was hard. Soon Amir was tired of the tears and he had no problem telling me how he felt. It was easy for him to forget because that child was not growing inside of him. For me, it was different. I rubbed my empty stomach and I cried, and I cried some more. I wished I had his support because grieving alone was exhausting. Yet again, this was another thing I had to figure out alone. During my grieving process, I began evaluating my life, the pregnancy, and my loss. I came to the hard truth that the stress of my job was contributing to the unhappiness I felt. As hard as it was, and I have no medical proof of this, but I believe the toxic work environment and the stress of my job had something to do with me losing my baby. They did genetic testing on the baby and found nothing wrong with him. Being home for two weeks gave me a lot of time to think. If I wanted another baby and not another occurrence like the I one had experienced, I had to make some life changes.

I don't know why this is the case, but many women experience miscarriages, but it's just not talked about. Many women suffer their loss in silence. According to the March of Dimes, in the U.S. there are more than four million confirmed pregnancies each year and between 10–20 percent of those pregnancies end in miscarriage. Miscarriage is the spontaneous loss of a pregnancy before the 20th week. I have experienced three miscarriages, but losing a baby at 16 weeks was heartbreaking. Ladies, I have no idea why there is such a silence around miscarriage. If you are a woman who experienced a miscarriage or several miscarriages, my advice is for you not to do what I did. I didn't seek the professional help that I needed to deal with my grief. I don't know why I didn't seek help, but handling my grief alone was exceedingly difficult.

On May 31, 2006, I returned to work and had a meeting with my boss. I requested to become a field employee. This would cut down on my four-hour-per-day commute, and working out of my home would physically take me out of the toxic work environment that I was a part of. The arrangement I negotiated was to work out of my home three days per week and the other two days onsite, at a government building for one of the projects I had. Working remotely was one of the best decisions I had made for my family. I had more time to spend with my son, to do little things for myself, and to juggle the demands of family and work. My heart was yearning for another child. I was determined to lose the weight I put on during the pregnancy, to get my body in optimal shape. I found ways to deal with my grief that did not involve food. After I lost the weight I put on while pregnant, we started trying again for another baby.

October 5, 2006

I'm pregnant! The Lord does answer prayers, and he has granted me my wish. This time, however, unlike my past pregnancies I had to take the test to know I was pregnant. In past pregnancies my swollen boobs were a dead giveaway. This time they are not swollen at all. I missed my period, but last month I was a little late so that wasn't alarming. I figured it was due to my weight loss. I have been getting headaches and experiencing light headedness, so I took the test. I'm so happy, yet so scared at the same time. I guess I would feel more confident if I had some of the same symptoms like in past pregnancies. But I know each pregnancy is different, so I need to just relax. I have an appointment at Johns Hopkins for October 18 and 20, so pretty soon I will

get checked out. I also managed to lose 19 pounds, so I am
starting out this pregnancy at a much lower weight than the
previous one, and I am happy about that. I know I need to let
go and let God. He will take care of both of us.

I was apprehensive about my pregnancy, so before I shared
the news with family and friends, I wanted to get past the 20-
week mark because of what happened with my last pregnancy.
Being a field employee, I did not see my work colleagues, so
that made it an easier task. People don't know what to say
to a woman who has experienced a miscarriage. While they
meant no harm, some of the comments people said to me after
my miscarriage were insensitive.

I wanted to give this baby every possible chance of survival,
so I made the decision to return to Johns Hopkins Hospital
for my care throughout the pregnancy. A remarkable thing
happened during this pregnancy—the Crohn's disease stayed in
remission. It was almost as if I didn't have the disease anymore.
I experienced zero Crohn's symptoms. This pregnancy was
so different from what I experienced with my first one. I could
eat whatever I wanted, and I remained active throughout the
entire pregnancy.

In the midst of working full-time remotely and taking care of
Sebastien, I helped Amir with his dream of being a business
owner. From our early days of dating, he had always talked
about that business he would own one day. Amir decided that
he wanted to open a Dollar Store. While it was difficult timing,
I helped with the planning and marketing. I had zero interest in being a business owner, but I wanted to support Amir.
Starting a retail business was Amir's brainchild. I supported
him financially, and he handled the day-to-day operations. We
started with one location; later, Amir expanded and opened
a second store.

Today is the big day for my ultrasound. Of course, getting through the day was difficult because my appointment was at 3 p.m. I had plenty to keep me busy. Things have been moving along with the store. The packages have begun to arrive, so this effort is getting more real every day. I know that the next couple of weeks will be difficult but once the store gets setup, things will slow down a bit. I know that in the beginning it will be hectic until we figure out ways of doing things and iron out the kinks. Drum roll please...We are having another little boy! It was great seeing him move around, open his mouth, and put his hands up to his face. When I got home, I showed Sebastien the baby pictures and told him that this was his baby brother and he said, "Mommy, I love my baby brother." That was just so cute. I will be the only woman in a house full of men and testosterone. He is measuring right on time, and everything seems o.k. with him from the ultrasound. That is the best news that I could possibly receive.

Another Setback—Can They Do That?

I am accustomed to setbacks, and throughout this pregnancy, I was fully prepared for a medical setback. But the one that I experienced surprised me. This was heartbreaking because I didn't believe that a company could be so mean, with utter disregard for people who work for them. At that time, I've put in more than seven years into the company, and one month before my maternity leave, they made me part-time. This was such a blow because they were not guaranteeing me 20 hours of work per week. They told me they would have to keep everyone in the office busy and if any work was left over, they would send some my way. As a result, I lost all my benefits: medical, dental and 401K. They didn't let me go, so I was unable to collect unemployment. There was no severance, and all I received was my unused vacation. The most hurtful part about all this was that it was obviously carefully orchestrated.

I did not tell anyone at work that I was pregnant because I was fearful of a miscarriage. As a full-time field employee, I was not required to go into headquarters. We had a team-building event in early March, and I was required to attend. That was when my boss and coworkers saw that I was pregnant. A few weeks later on March 23rd, my boss called to inform me that they were making me a variable part-time employee. Was that a coincidence? You be the judge of that.

I contacted an attorney to explore the possibility of legal action. What I found out surprised me. The lawyer told me the burden of proof was on me and that pregnancy discrimination cases were difficult to win. She wanted me to find someone who worked at the company who could attest to the fact that I was denied work because I was pregnant. Realistically, I couldn't ask anyone to jeopardize their job for me, and no one would agree to that. Unfortunately, this was not the first time this company did something like that. They did it to a former boss of mine, another woman of color, while she was pregnant. I had to let this go because without a job, I did not have the $375 hourly rate the lawyer was requesting to pursue my case. I decided that I was going to spend my energies focused on the upcoming birth of my son and to take care of my family. It's unfortunate that a company can get away with such unscrupulous behavior. I'm sure it happens more frequently than we realize.

Ladies, get ready because there are many inequalities in the workplace. You may experience some because of your gender and/or race. If you are a woman in the workforce and you haven't experienced any kind of inequality, whether it be pay equity or promotion, please consider yourself lucky. This is the society we live in, and while it's not fair, the more prepared you are to recognize it when it's happening to you, the better equipped you will be to handle it. My advice is to fight those inequalities when you can, but if you're unable due to your circumstances, find a way to cope and move on. That's what I did.

Life came full-circle, and I was yet again fortunate that I had my mom with me during one of the most difficult times of my marriage. I have heard of immigrants who migrate to the United States and "migrate" away from their families, meaning they never looked back—they never lent a helping hand, and essentially, they forgot where they came from or who helped them along the way before they migrated. Fortunately, I was never one of those immigrants. I kept a strong bond with my mom and extended family and helped them in any way I could. These ties served to help me when I was most vulnerable and in the greatest need.

May 17, 2007

Today, my Mom came from Jamaica to help us for the next six months. I am so grateful that she is giving up such a long time to help out with her grandsons. It's good to see her and Sebastien. He's just so happy to see his Nana. The pregnancy is going well, and the baby dropped because I can really feel him. Today at my 37 weeks checkup I was four centimeters dilated. I am just so happy that the baby is now full-term. Since Sebastien came at 36 weeks, I was fearful that Emilien would come early also. Well, he can come anytime now, and I am just so happy he made it to full term. My doctor wants me to get to 38 weeks, and after that we can talk about inducing if the baby doesn't get here. I am so exhausted these days.

I know that I am doing way too much for how pregnant I am, but the store is making us all work like crazy. My goal was to get the upstairs done before I have the baby, but there is just so much to do. I don't believe that is possible right now. I guess all I can do is just get as much done as possible.

On Friday, May 25, 2007, my son, Emilien, made his entrance into the world, weighing in at 6 pounds 14 ounces and 19.5 inches in length. This was a much easier pregnancy and a much easier delivery. Amir and I arrived at Johns Hopkins Hospital at 9:30 a.m., and at 5:47 p.m. I gave birth to my son. Don't get me wrong; the labor was the same intense pain, but Emilien made his entrance more quickly than his brother. It was a joy to hold Emilien in my hands right away. He was perfect. After worrying about his safety for so long, it was good to spend the time bonding with my son. The intense joy I felt for this boy can only be described as pure love. I was praying for a little girl, but I believe God sent me this little boy because I lost my other son. I am a true testament to the power of prayer. The Lord heard my prayers. Was everything perfect in my world? Far from it. As the higher wage earner in the family, I was now unemployed with two children and in a marriage that had lost its luster a long time ago.

May 26, 2007

I didn't sleep much last night. I guess it has to do with the excitement of having my son, and the pain I am feeling afterwards, but now I am truly exhausted. I have to get some rest before I get out of this hospital because there is nothing at home waiting for me but work. Emilien is nursing well. I can't see what he's getting, but the nurses assure me that he's getting something. I can't believe my husband didn't even have the decency to call me after he left the hospital. I called his cell phone twice last night and no response. I called home at midnight, and he still wasn't there. My goodness, I just had his baby and instead of going home so that Sebastien can see one of his parents, he is out doing his own thing. I called my Mom and she said Sebastien doesn't want to go to sleep because he's waiting on daddy. What in the world could be more important to him than his family? I am tired. I am tired of arguing with him about his late-night trips. I am tired of feeling all alone in this marriage. I am tired of feeling like I am raising our kids by myself. At this time, I should feel pure joy after the birth of our son, but again he has robbed me of that. I feel so depressed right now, but I hope it gets better.

After I had my son, I started looking for employment. I was in a more fortunate position than many other immigrants who might be in similar situations. As a United States citizen, I could now look anywhere for employment because my status was no longer linked to my job, like it was when I had my H-1B visa and was tied to the company that got rid of me. What would I have done if I were still on an H-1B visa? I would have had to find a new company to sponsor me. Those situations are harder when trying to secure employment, especially in the recession that was happening in 2007–2008. That was one of the times in my life when I was fortunate to be an American.

Another benefit for me as an American citizen occurred on November 4, 2008, when, for the first time, I could exercise my right to vote. I know there are Americans who don't vote, while there are immigrants like me who fought really hard for the right to vote. Voting means a lot to immigrants who are happy for the privilege of being accepted and for making this country our own. And what a year to be voting. I never thought that I would experience such a historic event when the United States elected its first Black President. I was proud to cast my vote because it was historic on numerous fronts. This was an experience I never wanted to forget. I took my Sebastien with me to vote. He was only four years old at the time, and

I know he will never remember how I was ranting and raving about the importance of voting. In my mind, I kept thinking that Martin Luther King, Jr.'s speech "I have a dream that my four little children will one day live in a nation where they will not be judged by the color of their skin but by the content of their character..." was finally coming to fruition in our society. My son and I shared this historic moment. I brought him in the polling station with me, and I lifted him up so that he could help me pull down the ballot for President Barack Obama. I believed that America was making a turning point where all citizens are created equal.

Life Lessons From This Chapter:

- As a woman of color, I will have to fight for the career I want—there will be inequalities, but I can't let that stop me; I have to keep fighting.

- The joining of a man and a woman in marriage can be a beautiful thing—however, you can be married and still be alone.

- Don't blindly accept what the medical professionals tell you—be an active participant in your care.

- Never give up. I had faith that one day I would become an American citizen, and despite challenges, it happened.

- The Lord is a way maker and a miracle worker— we must have faith in Him.

CHAPTER 5

WHEN THE WALLS CAME CRASHING DOWN

"You can gain strength, courage, and confidence by every experience in which you really stop to look fear in the face. You are able to say to yourself, 'I lived through this horror. I can take the next thing that comes along!'"

—Eleanor Roosevelt

When it all comes tumbling down, how do you survive? How about when children are part of the equation? How does a woman help herself while protecting her children? As an immigrant, I know very well what it feels like to have nothing. On the other hand, I also know what it feels like to have enough to cover all my needs and still have an abundance to experience life's luxuries, such as fancy cars, vacations, and a closet full of the types of clothes I want. I went from six people living in a small three-bedroom home growing up to owning and living in a 6,000-plus-square-foot home on two acres of land with a cow pasture as a neighbor. For an immigrant, that is the epitome of accomplishing the American dream. When you lose everything, you can either wallow in self-pity or you can pick yourself up, dust yourself off, and keep striving.

When it comes to relationships, I've made a lot of mistakes. But who hasn't? I can sum up my mistakes in one word—naivete. When I left my homeland, I was determined to succeed, and nothing was going to get in the way of that. I was laser-focused on my goal. For the most part, I kept my head down in those books while the world passed me by. During those formative early adulthood years when it's important to learn by trial and error, I was not doing any of those learnings. I lacked real-life experiences when it came to dealing with the opposite sex. I'm a classic case: I attended an all-girls institution for five years of high school, I grew up in a church with strong instructions to keep away from boys, and my fear of an unwanted pregnancy became the icing on the cake to keep boys/men at bay. I dated casually and had a few boyfriends, but it was not until I was a senior in college that I felt relaxed enough to fully embrace a committed relationship. My lack of experience was front and center, and while I was looking for love and commitment, he was not.

During the early dating phase, Amir could do no wrong! He was thoughtful of my needs, helpful, and did the things a boyfriend should do to seal the deal. He offered to pick my mom up from Baltimore Washington International Airport and drive her two hours to Pennsylvania for my graduation. He drove two hours once per month to spend the weekend with me in Pennsylvania, and he was present for all the major school events, Valentine's dance, and senior socials. These are just a few examples of some of the wonderful things that he did. What I didn't recognize at the time, but clearly written in black and white, were the controlling tendencies that started from the beginning of this relationship.

There were red flags, but I could not see them for what they were. Ladies, if your man forgets your birthday, that is a red flag. Let me tell you what happened to me. The first time Amir forgot my birthday, we had been dating for a year. He did not apologize; he told me that I was overreacting and that it wasn't a big deal. The next year, he forgot again. Amir continued to forget my birthday year after year. After all, the date never changed, so how hard was it for him to not remember? Initially, I made excuses for him. I tried to convince myself that since I was all the way in South Carolina, it just slipped his mind. This behavior did not change when we lived together. I had to remind him every year when it was my birthday. My close family and friends all over the world remembered and acknowledged my birthday, but my husband didn't. Ladies, don't ignore red flags because these behaviors tend not to change.

Ironically, why couldn't I recognize that every argument became my fault? No one is perfect, but it always seemed that I was the imperfect one. I started questioning myself— *I have a temper that I need to control. I'm making him angry. I'm causing him to do the things he is doing.* It was always my fault, and Amir was blameless. I had some legitimate concerns, but they were always swept away with the right words, an act of kindness, or a great spin to somehow make it my fault. Even during this time, I considered myself a strong Black woman. However, I was no match for Amir's manipulation that began at the onset of our relationship. Our dating for three years long-distance contributed to not fully getting to know the man with whom I was in a relationship. The thing about long-distance relationships is that you are in the "honeymoon" phase for long periods, which means that when the couple gets together, both parties try to be on his/her best behavior. Once we moved in together, I noticed a different side to the man whom I had invested a lot of time in. The biggest bone of contention between us was his unfaithful tendencies. Now, looking back, I can call it exactly what it was—the man was never faithful to me, and I was too young and "dumb" not to notice what was clearly right in front of me.

I watched my mom go through a marriage with infidelity and disrespect, and I vowed to myself that I would never put up with that from any man, but I did. At first, he always had an excuse for his whereabouts. His explanations were all plausible, and he started convincing me that these things were in my head and that I just didn't know how to handle a good thing. Living in the same space, the things that could be explained away when I was far away in South Carolina were now difficult to do when we were around each other day in and day out. For some reason, this man always seemed to have female "friends" whom he needed to do this or that for, even at the expense of our own relationship. Having a conversation about these areas of concern always resulted in it somehow being my fault.

October 24, 1999

It seems as if I am living through a nightmare. The man that I have loved for three long years seems to be slipping out of my grasp, and there is nothing I can do about it. Last night some woman named Edith showed up at our door again for a night on the town with my man. What does that say to me? Of course, he doesn't respect me nor my feelings. What more can I do or say? I blew up because I was hurt and shocked that he would do something like this so soon after we discussed it last weekend. Amir says that nothing is going on between him and Edith. If that were the case, why can't he cut it off? My point exactly since this thing with Edith is causing me so much grief. To complicate matters, we were scheduled to move into our new house in five days. I can't eat nor sleep because all this stuff has consumed me. I don't know where things stand right now. His behavior is saying, there is no relationship; we are just two business associates buying a house together. What has become of us? I blame myself for so many things. I have become so weak and needy that Amir feels as if I can't live without him. Just the cold way in which he has been treating me leads me to believe that there are a lot of issues going on with him. Well, what do I do? I know I am insecure, but I don't have to put up with this. I am young, intelligent, beautiful, and I have a good heart. If Amir doesn't want me, then to hell with him. This whole situation might not be all negative. Now, time can give me an opportunity to pick up the pieces of my life and start living for Sidoney again. I have been trying so hard to be what Amir wants me to be, and in that process, I lost the strong, fighter instincts that have taken me so far in life. I am only 24 years old, and I have my whole life ahead of me. If Amir is for me, then we will be together; if not, then I will just move on with my life like I have done before. Don't get me wrong because I know it won't be easy, but I have people who love me and that is all that matters. It's time to stop feeling sorry for myself. Start dieting and working out to lose those unwanted pounds. Start pursuing activities that make me happy. Going out, having a good time is what it is about.

You guessed it, there were more situations with ladies who were just "friends." I should have known better. I could no longer trust my instincts. I hung in there because I kept telling myself I had a good man. Ladies, always follow your instincts because it will never steer you wrong. I should have run for the hills when I realized his controlling ways and discovered his infidelities. I stayed, but why did I stay? It can't be because we bought a house together. That could have easily been sold, and we could have split the proceeds. I stayed because I loved this man. In no time, we were back on the mends after every disagreement. This became an unbreakable cycle, and I clung on to Amir's promises of the great life we would have together. All thoughts of our rocky road were behind us, or so I thought. When he proposed, I should have handed back the ring and said, "No, thank you," but I didn't. Many women, including me, are of the belief that marriage solves everything, and that once they get married, all of the problems that they had before will miraculously disappear. I am here to tell you from experience that marriage doesn't solve everything, and I don't think your man will change once you have a ring on your left finger. After the proposal, with renewed optimism, I spent a year and a half planning my dream wedding. As a couple, the bulk of that time should have been spent preparing for our marriage and not just for a one-day wedding event. Looking back, we had no business getting married. I wanted forever; he wanted the next prettiest one who came along. I wanted a simple life; he wanted the high life. I loved him, but he loved what I could do for him. Talk about incompatibility at its finest.

Today, I can see that very clearly. We do a lot of things in the name of love. One of the greatest lessons I have learned is that love is not supposed to hurt. Love is not supposed to make you feel bad about yourself. Love is not supposed to make a woman shed so many tears. Love is not supposed to be unkind. A man who loves you will never disrespect you. Any man whom you have to make excuses for how he treats you is a clear indication that love is not part of that equation. The Bible tells us all we need to know about love. I read these scriptures many times, but sadly, I didn't evaluate them when I was in my situation.

1 Corinthians 13:4-7 (NIV)

Love is patient, love is kind. It does not envy, it does not boast, it is not proud. It does not dishonor others, it is not self-seeking, it is not easily angered, it keeps no record of wrongs. Love does not delight in evil but rejoices with the truth. It always protects, always trusts, always hopes, always perseveres.

What I was calling love was not love. A marriage license does not equate to love. A piece of paper will not guarantee you that someone will love you. I learned the hard way that someone who professed to love me brought the most hurt and pain in my life. I spent 14 years with Amir, and we were married for seven of those years. The walls began to crumble in 2007 when I was lost my job one month before my maternity leave began. We had ongoing issues of infidelity and verbal abuse, but the truth about why Amir wanted someone like me became very apparent. As a college-educated woman with two degrees, Amir realized my earning potentials from the day he met me.

He was a calculating individual. Nothing he did was by accident; everything was done for a purpose. While I had stars in my eyes about love, his stars were dollar signs. Our situations were different. I was college-educated, and he was not. He knew that one day I would have a decent income, and that would be of great benefit to him. I always earned more than Amir. In 2007, when my company laid me off, I was earning double what he did. His carefully laid-out plan came to a halt when that income was no longer coming into the household. Amir was a big talker of the future our family would have from all the business ventures he was pursuing, and I bought into it. He was doing all this for his family, or so he led me to believe. Why else would he be doing all this? I worked the money and put it in the account, and Amir spent most of it. In addition to covering our living expenses, a large chunk was going to business dealings in a country in West Africa that I had never been to. It became a constant source of argument between us when I wanted to buy something, and no money was in our account, or I was told this money was earmarked for something in Africa, with no discussion or further explanation.

Motherhood changed me. I became fiercely protective of my children and their needs. I was no longer satisfied as to why my children had to do without so I could financially support something I could not see. He accused me of not supporting his dreams, of not supporting the future of the family, and for being selfish. I was financially supporting all those things as I saw my hard-earned paycheck walk out the door. However, that did not stop the accusations. The loss of my income brought a new reality to our doors. No longer was there surplus money to support business ventures in a faraway land. Amir saw a significant drop in his paycheck when he had to put the family on his health plan. Interestingly, I carried him on my health plan for seven years, and I never complained once. He made sure I knew that he was not happy that his paycheck was being used to take care of health insurance for me and the kids. I was a saver and had put away $20,000 in savings in my personal account. Initially, I continued to put money in our joint account for household bills, but it was no longer the influx that I did while I was employed. Amir did some snooping and found a statement for my personal account, and he lost it. He demanded that I put the same amount of money in our joint account as I did while I was employed. As you can imagine, that resulted in a massive argument. I had no idea when I would get a job due to the recession. I thought it would be a better idea to put a pause on his business dealings overseas so that we could hold on to as much cash as we could until I got a job. He did not agree, and the arguing was non-stop.

He wanted none of my suggestions, and his controlling tendencies took over. It was either do it his way or there would be no peace in our household with the constant bickering. Like always, to bring peace, I went along with what he wanted. In eight months, my entire savings was completely wiped out, and I still hadn't found a job. During that time, it became apparent that while I was working and could provide him with all the money he needed, we were on better terms. When I wasn't working, the verbal abuse increased. All the money in the past that I worked for to allow him to pursue a business in the U.S. and overseas meant nothing. I was living in hell, but what choices did I have? I had a newborn, a three-year-old, and no job.

For the first time in my life, I felt stuck. There was nothing I could do but to continue searching for jobs. I developed postpartum depression after having my youngest, and I couldn't shake the depression. I believe the challenges of my marriage, the financial strain, and the lack of control over my situation were greatly impacting my depressive state. I had two young children to care for, I was working twelve-hour days in our retail store, I was trying to find a job in my field, and I was dealing with an unhealthy marriage. No wonder I was depressed. There was a lot of verbal abuse. He accused me of being lazy, not wanting to work, and wanting to live off him. During one of our numerous arguments, Amir said to me, "You are nothing. You are like the dust of the earth." Why would a husband make such disparaging remarks to his wife? Ladies, I will tell you why my husband saw nothing wrong with verbally abusing me—because he could and he had gotten away with it for years. While this was one of the worst that I experienced, I never checked him in ways that I should have in the past. So, in essence, he felt like he had the license to lash out at me in the worst possible way. I felt broken, and for the first time in my life, I began to question my worth. I felt like I let so many people down. I was supposed to come to the United States and achieve, but at that point in my life, I did not feel like an achiever. I felt like a woman with nothing—no job, no money, and no dignity.

The woman who fought hard to bring his children into the world and provide financial and emotional support to him was now his verbal punching bag. He did it because he knew there was nothing that I could have done in the state I was in. I love my children, and I wanted to hang on so that they could have an intact family; however, during that hard period, I didn't see a future for my marriage. I was just buying my time until my financial situation improved. I know the marriage vows that I took said, "For better or worse..." This was my worse, but I believe that God created me, and He always wants what is best for me, and this situation was not it.

The depression I was experiencing was real. I was never a big drinker because I didn't like how it made me feel. However, during this time, I found myself turning to alcohol to help dull the pain that I was feeling. Before that, I would occasionally have a drink; now, I found myself having a glass of Tia Maria, a dark liqueur made originally in Jamaica, with my antidepressant medication before I went to sleep several nights per week. Yes, it was only one glass of alcohol, but that was not my normal behavior.

December 29, 2007

Amir and I are really fighting. I knew this day was coming and now that it is here, I'm still not prepared for it. All of our savings are gone, and now comes the blame game. I know that Amir blames me for our financial state and the fact that I haven't worked in months. He said some pretty hurtful things to me, and I told him I would put back every penny that I took from our account to cover our bills and my portion. All in all, I took $6,000. I know I don't have that much money. But for now, I put $4,000 back, and I'm going to see if I can get the $2,000 any way that I can. Amir refused to acknowledge that if he had listened to me, we wouldn't be in this predicament right now. We argued when he decided to deplete our savings by sending $7,000 to Africa to work on the house there. He later withdrew an additional $6,000 from our account. He didn't even bother to ask me when he took the money and sent it back with his cousin who was visiting from Africa. He said $3,000 was to be used for the house project and $3,000 for his brother's funeral. With me *out of a job, I didn't think these were wise decisions. He blames me because he's trying to get a loan and is unable to qualify with his salary alone. He makes it seems like I want to stay home on my butt and do nothing. To make matters worse, when I got home this evening from working at the Dollar Store, I found a strange woman sitting in my kitchen holding my youngest child. I was furious of course, that he brought someone there and didn't let me know. He said he told me in the morning that he invited her. While he did, I thought that since I wasn't available that he would postpone the visit. It was not pretty. I was terribly angry because I told him on numerous occasions that I don't want anyone living in my house watching the kids. When I pushed back on her living with us, he insisted that she could still help us out with the kids. With no transportation, how does she plan on doing that? His response was that we can pick her up and drop her off. There was something not right with this scenario. I could feel it. We argued, and he told me I was "insecure" that I am nothing, I have no job, no money and I wanted to show off and not accept help. Of all the hurtful things that he said to me, an unfit mother was the hardest, and I don't know if I can forgive him for that. I feel so beaten down.*

Ladies, fight for what you know in your heart is right, even if you are in a toxic relationship. I had no doubt in my mind that the woman sitting in my kitchen who was supposed to be this great help to us was one of Amir's "friends" whom he wanted to move into our house. That man had lost his mind if he thought I would allow him to bring a stranger, "cousin" or not, to live in my house with me and my children. At that time, he felt that since he was the only one bringing in a paycheck, he had all the say. There was no way I was going to allow him to bring his infidelities under my roof. This was a non-negotiable for me. We fought hard, and he didn't speak to me for a month when I wouldn't agree. This, ladies, was worth fighting for.

When I became an American citizen, I now had the opportunity to file for my immediate family and sponsor a green card. As soon as I was able to, I filed for a green card for my mom. Amir and I had an argument about this because he wanted to know why I feel the need to file for her. I ignored him, and it turned out to be one of my best decisions. I was able to bring her to the U.S. to live with us and help me take care of the kids. Mom became a big help when I most needed her. Without a green card, she was on a visitor's visa, and she could not remain in the U.S. past six months at a time. However, with a green card, she could live permanently in the country.

Life came full circle. Leaving home at 16 years old meant that I didn't have a close relationship with my mom during my adolescent years, but I was fortunate that during this difficult time, Mom was with me. She came from Jamaica to help me right before my youngest son was born, and she stayed with me for six months. This was an invaluable help, not just with the children so that I could run the retail business, but she provided moral support as well. I was able to cry on her shoulders, and she served as a sounding board to help me as I was going through depression. As a mother, I know it was difficult for my mom to see her child going through such a tough time. She was in the house and witnessed Amir's verbal attacks. I would walk past her door sometimes after an episode and hear her crying. She felt powerless and didn't know how to help her child. But she didn't realize then just how much her mere presence meant to me. She was a pillar of strength, and I was able to get through that tough season in my life because of her help and support. Mom advised me to rely on my faith to keep me going. She stressed that I should continue reading my Bible and talking to God just like I talked to her. This became my motto, especially when she left to return to Jamaica.

The year 2008 saw some promises for me. I finally landed a lucrative position in my field and returned to the workforce. I was a broken person at that point in my life. I smiled outwardly, but inwardly I was truly hurting. I was sick of the fighting, sick of being in a loveless marriage, and sick of the financial challenges that we were experiencing. An interesting thing happened. Once I started making a decent salary again, things began to improve in our marriage and family. I took all of it with a grain of salt because I had been at the same place before, and it was always good for a period of time, but then it reverted back to the control and verbal attacks.

My situation was not the same this time around because I was a different person. I could not forget the hell I went through with Amir for that year that I was home without a job. I hesitate to use the word unemployed because I was working 12-hour days, managing two retail stores, and taking care of two small children. That was the hardest I'd ever worked in my entire life, but it just didn't come with a paycheck, nor was it appreciated by my spouse. Did I go to counseling? No. But I should have because I never dealt with the way I was treated. There are people in the Black community who don't believe in counseling. I am not one of those individuals. I didn't go because I had to make some tradeoffs. I didn't have the time to devote to counseling. I never forgot how Amir treated me during that year—the harmful words, the evil looks, and the demeaning way he treated me—all in the name of breaking me.

I slowly took my life back. I weaned myself off the antidepressant medication. The depressive state that I was in took a toll on my body as well. None of the work clothes I had fit me. I went shopping, and I stood in the middle of the store crying when the salesclerk brought me bigger and bigger size clothing to try on. I never lost sight of my goals to improve myself and my family situation. At that time, I didn't have a concrete plan, but the thoughts never left me. I began mulling over the question of what I could do to improve my life so that I could find happiness for myself and my children. I didn't want my boys to grow up in an unhealthy environment.

I was determined to get myself together. Despite the feelings of insecurity, I focused on my new job and got busy with the kids. Surprisingly, my situation started changing. My self-esteem was recovering, the pounds started coming off, and I began feeling more like my former self. For years, I prayed, and despite the mistreatments from Amir, I tried awfully hard to keep my family unit together. I always said that I didn't want my boys growing up in a broken home, so I sacrificed my own happiness just to keep them in a two-parent household. After I got a job and started being financially independent, the thought of leaving this situation that was not good for me physically, emotionally, nor spiritually, came across my mind again. But every time that thought came to my mind, I dismissed it. After all, that's what mothers do—we make sacrifices for our children. I kept hanging on for my boys' sake. However, at the start of 2009, I made my New Year's resolution like I did every year as a personal tradition. Looking back, that was the first year I did not make a resolution to work on strengthening my marriage. While my head was saying "stay," my heart was saying "go." My resolution became a self-fulfilling prophecy.

January 1, 2009

Sometimes it's exceedingly difficult for people to be brutally honest. I don't know if it's because of the start of another year, but I have to look at my life by taking the blinders off. If I want to be brutally honest, I have not been happy for an awfully long time. At 34 years of age, I can say that there is no passion in my life, no tenderness, and lately I don't even feel any love in my marriage. To be honest, it just seems like we are two roommates raising two kids. Do I want to continue in such a relationship? If I didn't have Sebastien and Emilien to consider I would have to make some different choices. I'm like any other woman; I want some romance in my life. I want to feel alive. So, since I lack all these things, and I just feel like I can't fight anymore, I'm going to let it go and focus on the things that I do have control over.

So, for 2009, this is the year for me! This is the year that I work on achieving that which will make me happy. With that said, here are my resolutions for 2009:

- Lose weight and adopt a healthy lifestyle.
- Put Sidoney first.
- Create a spiritual relationship with God.
- Work with Sebastien with reading and writing.
- Work on being a good mother to the boys.

The year started out as a very promising one; however, 2009 ended with great losses on more than one front: the loss of my older brother Carey and the loss of my marriage. Despite the losses, I finally got Sidoney back. I found the strength to do what was necessary to heal myself and to provide a better environment for my boys, one in which they saw love and not constant fighting. I began to put the boys and my needs before Amir's, and that made a lot of difference. Amir finally had to close down the two Dollar Stores because we were sinking financially and could not cover the mountain of debts that were coming in. As you can imagine, I had a fight on my hands. I was no longer willing to put my hard-earned cash into a sinking business. It was evident to me that something had to give, and I prioritized my family over his need to be seen as a businessman. Amir was the idea person, so when it came to a plan to dig us out of the financial mess, it rested on my shoulders. Godmom lent us $65,000 to cover all the debts that we had accumulated, and we shut down the business. While it was humiliating to have to go to her with my problems, I wasn't worried about repaying the loan because we had well over $100,000 worth of merchandise and equipment that we could sell and pay her back. At that time, I was becoming increasingly disgusted with the man I married because of his greed. Not many people would make the decision to lend someone $65,000, but Godmom did. Yet Amir could not be satisfied. After we received that money, he wanted me to go back to her and ask for an additional $50,000. For what, I'm sure you're wondering. Drum roll please...he wanted the money to complete the property he was building in West Africa. I adamantly refused, and that started another round of fighting. When he decided to go to Godmom himself, I gave her the heads-up, so she was well prepared to turn him down.

Losing my brother was heartbreaking. A month prior to his death, we were told that Carey needed open-heart surgery to replace the aortic valve in his heart that was not functioning properly. Five days after surgery, on October 2, 2009, Carey left this earth. This shook me to my core. Carey, my special needs brother, and I were remarkably close. It was a difficult trip for me to make back to Jamaica after being away for three years.

God does not make mistakes, and everything happens in His timing. While men are planning, God always has a different plan. I had to decide very quickly to head to Jamaica to take care of the burial for my brother. At the time, Amir was on his annual trip to West Africa where he typically remains for six weeks every year, "taking care of business." When Carey died, Amir had two weeks left on his trip. I explained about my brother's death and asked him to change his ticket and return home so that I could head to Jamaica. His response did not surprise me because he never went out of his way to help anyone, not even his wife and children. The boys were five and two years old at the time, and I was having difficulties getting someone who would watch both of them for two weeks until Amir returned to the United States. I had a difficult decision to make, and I ended up splitting the boys apart. It was a difficult transition, especially for Sebastien who had never been separated from his brother for such a long period. A neighbor kept Sebastien so he could continue going to school, and a family member of Amir kept Emilien.

As I prepared for my departure to Jamaica, I began paying our bills and was fervently searching for a bill in the office Amir and I shared. What I discovered was the catalyst that gave me the strength to leave this toxic relationship. Amir had compromising photos of himself and several different women. These appeared to be photos taken from his various annual trips to West Africa. Most shocking, one of the photos was taken during the first year of our marriage when we were at our "happiest." Even way back then, he was disrespecting me and not honoring his wedding vows. What does a wife do in a situation like this? I didn't have a manual, and this was not part of the pre-marital counseling. Ladies, I didn't have time on my hands to carefully plan out a course of action. However, I was no fool, and I knew I needed to do something that could help me when the marriage dissolved. I made copies of the compromising photos and put back the originals in their hiding place. Heading to Jamaica and putting my brother to rest had to be my focus. I tucked the discovery in the back of my mind.

Being in Jamaica and going through the process of planning my brother's funeral was a devastating time for me. I had to put aside my marital problems to be strong for my mom who needed me. Carey was only 36 years old, by all counts an incredibly young man. Mom was having a hard time handling the passing of her firstborn. The roles were reversed; now I had to be a pillar of strength for her. She had been there for various challenges in my life, and this was the time for me to do everything I could to help her heal. I didn't have any experience in planning a funeral; this was my first. To top it off, I was not versed in making such arrangements in Jamaica. I learned quickly by asking questions and took the lead in planning the homegoing service. I didn't have time to deal with my own feelings of loss because I was busy being the doer. Not until I sat down to write Carey's eulogy did it hit me that I wouldn't see my brother again. Sitting down and capturing his life on paper provided some peace. Standing up in front of a packed church was another story. I broke down on that day as I tried to deliver my carefully crafted message. I got through it but barely. As I struggled through the funeral, I was reminded of Carey's six-month visit to my home in 2007. My special needs brother was so much wiser than his baby sister. Despite his challenges, while he was with me, he told me that Amir was not a good man. My sign language was rusty from years of not practicing, so I struggled to communicate with Carey. He never gave up and made sure I understood what he was trying to tell me, that I had to get away from the bad man (he was referring to Amir). When he left this world, Carey saved me. If Carey had survived the surgery and couldn't function, Mom would have had to remain in Jamaica to take care of him and would not have been able to help me. I was comforted that even in death, my brother was protecting me!

On the plane ride back to the States, I began to reflect on the discovery that I had made of Amir's infidelity. What should I do? How should I handle the confrontation? I was most concerned with how I could protect my boys. How do you confront a habitual cheater? Granted, this was the first time that I had solid proof in my hands, but a woman always knows. Deep down,

I knew for years that he was not being faithful. I had confronted him numerous times, but he just threw them all back at me, saying I was insecure, starting problems, and just didn't want him to have fun with his friends. What married man who leaves work at 7 p.m. comes home regularly at 3 a.m.? Where was he until those hours of the morning? When I asked my husband about his whereabouts, I never got a plausible answer.

I confronted Amir the day I got back from Jamaica. I had a time crunch, so I knew I had to act quickly because I was due to be in London for a two-week business trip. This time, when I confronted Amir, his reaction was not exactly what I expected. He flipped the switch and asked me if I had ever cheated since we were married. He began with the avoidance technique; I guess he was buying some time because he didn't know what I had. I imagine this confrontation felt different for him. I was very calm; there was no arguing and no tears. I had nothing else to lose, and in that instance, I had to love Sidoney more than I loved him. I was hoping that he would at least tell me the truth. When it was clear that wasn't happening, I explained to him that before he created the perfect lie, I had proof of his infidelity. Amir lost it and accused me of invading his privacy. I couldn't believe what I was hearing. Your wife has proof of your infidelity and you want to talk about invasion of privacy? His reaction was that of a man accustomed to being in charge and controlling every situation. He had no more control over me, so his dramatic responses did not faze me. I had already devised an exit strategy, and the discussion we were having was only for me to tell him. Believe it or not, Amir beat me to the punch, and he was the one who asked me for a divorce.

While I can't be sure this is true, I have a theory about the chain of events that led to him asking for a divorce: one, I caught him by surprise; two, he needed to control the situation; and three, he did not expect my reaction. Amir knew that I didn't want the boys to be a product of a broken home, that I wanted them to grow up in a home with both parents. I believe he was counting on that when he asked for the divorce. He thought I would ask him to reconsider for the boys' sake. He thought I would recommend counseling so that we could work on our issues and keep the family together. He thought that would give him the upper hand because I would be emotional over the dissolution of our marriage. What he didn't know was that I had all the ammunition I needed to end this marriage. Even if I had considered working on our issues, but I wasn't, the evidence I found sealed the deal for me to get away from this man whom I was with for 14 years but didn't really know. I had four days to handle everything before my departure. I had an amazing colleague and friend, my assistant Linda, whom I confided in at work about the end of my marriage.

I was placed on a stretch project with high visibility in the company. The project required frequent trips to London; lots of work, sometimes 60-plus-hour weeks; and attention to detail. Despite the turmoil of my personal life, I knew I could successfully execute the project. I had no concerns about my abilities; however, I was nervous to let senior management know about my situation because I feared that I would be taken off the project. After all, it was high profile, and failure was not an option. I feared they would question my ability to manage my personal life with my work obligations. I needed this project and the success that would come with it. I also knew that this could result in a promotion. I shared my concerns with Linda about the project, so she kept it confidential. She was of immense help to me. I needed a place to keep some valuables, and she held on to them for me.

Linda was the one who told me about the Employee Assistance Program (EAP) that my job provided free of charge. Through EAP, I was provided the names of divorce lawyers. I contacted one and was lucky enough to get an appointment two days later. Why did I need a divorce attorney so quickly? I did some snooping and found out that Amir had grand plans. It appeared that he was looking for mansion-style homes to rent in his West African country. Why would he need to rent a massive home there? I drew my own conclusions and was scared that he might take my children away and return to West Africa to live. Since I was leaving the United States on business travel for two weeks, I wanted to ensure that I was armed with the right information before my departure. The meeting with the lawyer was one that I will never forget.

Before all this, I had never met with a lawyer for anything other than my immigration filing status, and that was just to sign a few papers. I told the lawyer everything I knew and my concerns about him taking the boys overseas. What the lawyer revealed was something out of a soap opera, and I couldn't believe it was happening to me. I remember the lawyer asking me two questions: "How is your credit?" and "Do you believe your husband is a criminal?" My response was that I had excellent credit. I tried not to hyperventilate about the criminal question because I was scared. It turned out that Amir was not a "criminal." However, my excellent over-800 credit score that I had was a thing of the past and a figment of my imagination. Amir had stopped paying the mortgage and our house was in foreclosure proceedings, he had borrowed over $100,000 in credit card debt in both our names, and my credit score was now in the toilet. How could this happen to me?

I only had one credit card that I paid off in full every month. I went to the lawyer with one problem and left with a tsunami which was now my life. I'm sure by now you understand why the reverse psychology Amir was using to deal with our situation would never work because I simply knew too much. Why would he jeopardize the home that we live in with our children? Where did all the mortgage and credit card money go? One answer:

West Africa! When he asked for the divorce, I said okay and got a pad of paper. I wrote both our names down and began dividing our assets on that sheet of paper, which was to Amir's horror because that was not what he was expecting. It was difficult to leave for two weeks while all this was going on, but in retrospect, it was for the best because it gave me time away to think and plan. Thankfully, Mom came back from Jamaica to watch the children for me. I left her with two instructions before I left for London: pack and pray.

You see, people like Amir always have a plan. But while he had a plan, the God that I served had an even bigger plan. I believe the Lord led me to those compromising photos. He knew what my Amir was planning, and He was taking care of me. Sometimes when you are in challenging situations, you begin to question God. "Why me, God?" I did exactly that. To be honest, I had been angry with God for a long time. I did things the right way—I wasn't a promiscuous teenager, I didn't have children out of wedlock, I didn't do drugs nor get into trouble. I followed the right path. So, why me?

At that time in my life, I couldn't see that the Lord Jesus was saving me and that's why all these things needed to happen. You can't have a testimony if you don't have a test. And, boy, did I have a test. Ladies, some of you may be aware of the type of people who like to game the system. I not only knew one, but I was also married to him. During the economic downturn in 2008–2009, many families were losing their homes due to foreclosures. Many banks were offering loan modifications to help out people who were unemployed so that they could save their homes. Amir and I were not in that situation, but he got greedy, and despite my advice not to go down that route, he ignored me and proceeded. It was always Amir's way or no way. It was hard to watch Amir jeopardize the home that we built for our family. We had no money at that time, even though I was in a job that paid well and he also worked; we had nothing. Every time I turned around, my hard-earned money was being funneled to West Africa, to a country I had never visited.

Amir always had a plan. I don't believe he intended to lose the house, but when he realized that it was happening, he had a new bright idea. He wanted me to withdraw the $20,000 needed to pay the arrears on the house from my 401K, sell the house, and split the proceeds with him. The money in my 401K was all the money I had to my name. Of course, I declined his suggestion because I had no interest—we were over. He wanted to continue to use me to save a house that he made the decision to jeopardize. This is how I know that the God I serve was at the helm of all this. If I hadn't found the compromising photos that started this chain of events, I would have withdrawn all the money I had in my 401K to save the house so that my children would have a place to live. Amir knew I would do anything to protect my kids. However, the Lord Jesus saved me! At the time, I couldn't see it. My anger at God was misplaced, because while I thought He left and forgot about me, He was right there by my side every step of the way.

There was only one other time when I needed the Lord so badly, and that was when I was pregnant with Sebastien. I needed my mom to pray because financially I was ruined. I had nothing in the bank. In fact, I had gotten paid right before I left for Jamaica, and Amir, despite the $10,000 he took to West Africa with him, still felt the need to pull out additional money from our account while he was in West Africa. That was money that I was counting on to pay our bills. I was down to my last $20—with two small children, myself, and my mom to take care of.

Ladies, let me tell you about faith. My mom had strong faith that God would see us through. The Lord needed to pull off a miracle to get me out of this situation I found myself in. When my faith was wavering, Mom reminded me of the countless times in my life where the Lord came to my rescue. I told her to pack up our things because I was determined to move my family out of the situation as soon as humanly possible.

When I told her to pack, I had nowhere to move to, no money to pay the security deposit and first month's rent, and no money to pay movers. I'm hoping you can picture the scenario. During my two-week business trip in London, I hardly slept. I worked hard at my job, and I used every free moment planning and working on my exit strategy. I made a list of things I needed to take care of to untangle my life from Amir, and I was doing it on "steroids." I was moving to an area that was significantly more expensive than where I was living. I didn't know that they could ask for so much money to rent those houses I was looking at. I contacted a realtor, and I had properties to review when I got back. I could no longer afford private school for Sebastien, so I had to figure out how to register a child in the public school.

I wanted to move quickly because it was difficult to be around Amir after I discovered all his deceit. I could wait until I got a few paychecks to save the money so I could pay for the move, but I didn't. I picked up my phone and called Godmom, and she graciously offered to send me money to cover my immediate moving needs. If you've never had bad credit, let me enlighten you—people look at you differently. The intrusive questions that I received were embarrassing. My credit report was my "new report card," and it was not good. My new reality hit me with the house rental. I was constantly told that I had a good salary; however, because of my bad credit, they either did not want to rent to me or they required someone to co-sign with me. I had no idea that co-signing occurred on a rental property. I thought that only happened with loans. I swallowed my pride and called Godmom again and asked her to co-sign for me.

This was a low point for me. I knew she would never judge me, and she did everything in her power to help me get through the situation; however, I felt like I let her down. She got me to the United States, I successfully got my degrees, and up until that point, I'd always figured a way out, and this time I couldn't. She co-signed, and I was able to rent a home for my family.

December 4, 2009

Today is my 35th birthday, and it's a day for new beginnings. I have the best birthday present which is a new start. Today, I am scheduled to move out of the home that I built with Amir and have lived in for the past five years to start my new life as a single mother in my own place. Even though we have been packed up for a week, I was packing on faith because I only got the o.k. on the rental property yesterday. I did not tell Amir my actual moving date because I did not want any trouble. We had agreed that I would get the master bedroom set, and he has since changed his mind and now said he wants it. I am actually blessed because six of my colleagues from work came to help me unpack my belongings. They also brought pizza and juice, which was genuinely nice of them. I was truly overwhelmed by their generosity. They stayed until close to midnight. Needless to say, Amir was furious when he got home, and we were not there. It's unfortunate that I left in that manner, but I have to protect the children from unnecessary bickering and animosity.

Freedom felt great. I imagine that's how a prisoner feels when she is released and walks through the gates of a prison. I became a "prisoner" in my own life, and it wasn't until after I was out of the situation that I realized how great it felt to be free—free to live my life without criticism, chastisement, and someone who thought little of me and my abilities. I slowly got myself back.

Was it easy? Absolutely not. Something interesting happened when I began to relearn who I was. I had lost myself in that marriage. I had lost my fighter instincts and the inner strength that pushed a 16-year-old to pick up and move to a new country. Slowly, that person began to emerge, and it was right on time because I needed everything in me to fight for my children and the life I wanted them to have.

Getting a divorce is not for the faint at heart. I learned so much during the process, especially because Amir wanted a major fight. He was unrealistic and greedy. For those of us who are or were married, how many of us took the time before walking down the aisle to educate ourselves about divorce? Do we know what is involved in the process and how we can protect ourselves? I know I didn't. Maybe, this should be a helpful discussion during pre-marital counseling. After all, more than 50 percent of marriages in the United States end up in divorce. I found the process to be long, costly, and awful. The interesting thing is that our divorce should not have taken as long as it did because we had no assets that we were fighting over; there was no house, money in the bank, or luxury vehicles. What were we fighting over? We were mainly fighting over custody and child support of the children. Writing this has me cracking up because we were also in court fighting over a bedroom set!

Yes, even though we agreed that I would keep the master bedroom set and he would keep the set in the guestroom, and I had already moved, Amir was fighting me for it in court. Even his lawyer chuckled that he was fighting over a bedroom set. The children became our biggest bone of contention. It was always about money with Amir, so there was no surprise that he did not want to pay the amount of money that the court decided he should for child support. The way this works is that they put both parent's income into a database, and it spits out a figure that the non-custodial parent should pay. Amir was required to pay me $870 per month for both children. Because I earned significantly more than he did, that would cover 30 percent of the children's living expenses and I would be responsible for paying 70 percent. Any reasonable man would be fine with that, but not him. In fact, when he approached me to get rid of the lawyer, he offered to pay me $300 per month for both children.

Amir fired his lawyer one month into the process, so he was representing himself. Therefore, he didn't care how long he dragged out the process. When I left Amir, I did not receive any money for the children from him for four months until the court ordered him to pay. It's so ridiculous that we were fighting over the amount he was required to pay. When my lawyer got him to agree to $700 per month, I accepted it to avoid the costly legal fees. I had to weigh the cost of paying the lawyer $300 per hour to fight with my limited financial resources.

March 5, 2010

Last night, it was difficult for me to sleep. I began to have stomach issues, and I know that it is my nerves for the divorce status meeting in Hagerstown. I have never been in a courthouse so I was nervous as to what will occur. Our lawyers went into the judge's chambers for half an hour, and then they got out and took us to an adjacent conference room to iron out our differences. It was totally awful. Amir sat in front of me and lied, lied, and lied. He said I didn't give him any money to go to Africa in September, that I bought my mom a house with marital assets, that there is no viable property in Africa, and that he did not file or intend to file bankruptcy. He fought us on everything. He refused to pay child support from December to February, he refused to pay me my half of the money he received from selling the Dollar Store merchandise, and he was adamant in dropping the court mandate $870 per month for child support to $700. I'm sure he feels as if he was victorious, *but I can't deal with the fighting anymore. This guy is scum because he's only shortchanging his own children. Today was an exceedingly difficult day for me. I can't believe I was with this guy for 14 years.*

When it comes to the welfare of children, the court wants to ensure that they approve the situation that is best for them. I wanted full custody of the boys for two reasons: I was fearful of Amir taking the boys away to live in West Africa, and I knew I would have difficulties making decisions for the boys if we had joint custody because it would be Amir's way or no way. While I was willing to negotiate the child support amount, full custody was non-negotiable. We fought hard for months about custody. Amir wanted the children to live with me 90 percent of the time, but on paper, we would have joint custody. Joint to me sounds more like 50-50 but that would have to be the thinking of a rational person, and he was far from being reasonable.

For me, custody of my boys was worth moving heaven and earth for, if I needed to. I knew this man, and I was well aware that nothing meant more to Amir than money and his business ventures. So, when my lawyer was hitting roadblocks, I stepped in. Ladies, I've told you before that you need to fight for the things that are worth fighting for like your life depends on it. My lawyer tried various arguments to get Amir to agree to full custody, but none was successful until I told my lawyer exactly what he should use to get me the full custody.

During our mediation when we were putting the separation agreement together, both our lawyers put on the table what each of their clients wanted. My lawyer stated that he wanted half of the property and business that was in West Africa, and Amir's lawyer said there was no property. Clearly, he was unaware of what my lawyer was referring to. Lucky for me, I had documentation, which my lawyer produced, that backed up my claim. Now, this became marital assets that would need to be divided equally. I knew that Amir wanted me to get none of it, and I was willing to sacrifice that for full custody of my boys. When my lawyer was struggling with the custody battle, I told him to tell Amir that I would forego all claims to the property in West Africa if he would give me full custody. My lawyer was not happy with the direction that I wanted him to go. When I did a calculation, the amount of money spent on that venture was to the tune of over $800,000 USD throughout the course of our marriage.

I made this decision against the advice of my lawyer because I would have done anything to get full custody of my children. Also, the process the lawyer explained I would go through to get whatever the court awarded me was not something I was willing to do. Basically, if a judge in the United States awarded me half of a property in West Africa, I would have to go to that country, hire a lawyer there to help me get what I was due. I was not about to go to a country where I didn't speak their language to fight in court. I was not interested in more fighting; I wanted to move on with my life. Just like I predicted, once Amir was informed that I would give up all my claims to the property and business in West Africa, he agreed to give me full custody of our children.

My divorce took longer than a typical divorce because of the games Amir was playing. I started the divorce in Washington County, Maryland, and after paying $8,000 in legal fees and attending several hearings, a judge dismissed the case due to a lack of evidence on Amir's part. I had to start over and paid my lawyer more money to file a new case and represent me at my divorce hearing. After one year and three months, on March 3, 2010, I had my hearing and the divorce was granted in 15 minutes. I thought I would be happy and jumping for joy when this day came. Admittedly, I had mixed feelings. While I was happy that I was no longer tied legally to this man, more than 14 years was over in 15 minutes, and that made me sad.

Amir owed me four months of back child support. One thing the divorce made easier was the fact that I no longer had to wait for him to pay his child support when he felt like it. His paycheck would be garnished, and his child support payment would be directly deposited into my account every two weeks. The only money he would have to pay me directly was his half of out-of-pocket medical expenses for the boys. Not arguing over his child support payments was a blessing. I wish I could tell you that was my final court appearance with Amir. Since 2010, I've had to take Amir to court four times for nonpayment of medical bills. He refused to pay his portion of the bills when I presented them to him. I've always carried the boys on my medical and dental insurance, and per our divorce, Amir didn't have to reimburse me for half that money that comes out of my paycheck. Despite this, he still refused to pay his portion.

Amir is not the type of dad to provide any extras to his boys, except $100 each on their birthdays and every Christmas. Therefore, I had to ensure that I made the plans necessary to secure a future for the boys and me. I had some tough choices to make to set us up for financial success. I have always been good with money, a saver more than a spender. I am the type of person who creates and lives on a budget. When my lawyer gave me a printout of all the banks that I now owed money, I picked up the phone and started calling them. What I discovered and experienced was far from pleasant. For me, to be in a predicament where I had creditors coming after me was new territory. During that timeframe, credit cards would send attractive offers to people with good credit. When I received those offers, I did what I thought most sensible people would do in those situations, I ripped them up and threw them in the trash. Ladies, please pay attention, there is this thing called marriage that complicates financial issues, so please be aware. If your husband got a credit offer in the mail, addressed to both of you, and he called the company (all he needs is your social security number) and accepted the terms and received the money, he could do this without your consent. Would you call that fraud? What I began to learn very quickly throughout my ordeal was that there were different rules because I was married. In a nutshell, I couldn't fight any of these charges because it would be my word against Amir's. Frankly, the credit card companies didn't care; they just wanted their money.

When I began making those calls, I got scared because the creditors were threatening to garnish my paycheck and call my place of employment. After I reached everyone, just to make the minimum payment would be around $1,500 monthly. I knew I couldn't afford this, especially when I didn't benefit from the money they dished out to Amir. I told my divorce lawyer about my experience, and he recommended that I share what was happening with my employer and that I consider bankruptcy. I was initially against bankruptcy because of the stigma attached to it. However, I met with a lawyer and I swallowed my pride and filed for bankruptcy. I took a debtor education course, and my case was discharged. Sadly, my credit score dropped drastically because it now had a foreclosure and a bankruptcy on it. I kept moving in faith that one day my financial situation would turn itself around.

I thought my financial woes were behind me with the bankruptcy and foreclosure. However, a year and a half after filing a joint 2009 tax return with Amir, the last year we were together, he brought me some news that turned into being a setback that I did not need as I worked to improve my financial situation. The 2009 tax return was the last one that I filed with Amir. In retrospect, I made a big and costly mistake to the tune of $35,155. I should have known better. With all the things that

I discovered about Amir, running up over $100,000 in credit card debt in both our names, I should not have filed taxes with him. With all that was going on, when he contacted me about getting our taxes done, I didn't think he was going to do anything fraudulent. After all, while he messed with some credit cards, who in their right mind would mess with the IRS? He did, and unfortunately, he dragged me into the mess with him.

In 2009, we shut down our two retail businesses. When we were filing our taxes, Amir informed our accountant that the business experienced a $50,000 loss. I didn't question him because I knew that when the business shut down, there was over $100,000 worth of merchandise and equipment remaining. When I moved out, I took nothing with me and had no idea what he did with the merchandise that was in the basement when he eventually moved out of the house we shared. The IRS came knocking, and on August 6, 2011, Amir informed me that the IRS would like us to provide receipts to show the $50,000 business loss. I was livid when he informed me that he did not get a receipt when he sold $50,000 worth of merchandise for $3,000. I knew Amir was lying. The tax refund that we received as a result of this business loss needed to be returned, plus a year and a half of interest. I was angry, not only because of what Amir did, but because of my own stupidity. This was another financial blow to me. I was already paying back the loan that Godmom gave us, of which he never paid back his portion, and now this.

I explained everything to my new accountant and had to pay him $2,000 to help me clear up the mess I was in. I wanted to pay back the IRS half of the $30,000 debt but it doesn't work like that with the IRS. Since it was a joint tax return, both Amir and I were equally responsible for the repayment. I filed an innocent spouse petition since I was not the one responsible for the day-to-day running of the business. I wanted the IRS to split the liability so that I would be responsible for only half of the repayment.

The IRS denied that request, but I appealed and was granted a hearing. My accountant was confident that once I had an opportunity to present my case live, my request for separation of liability would be granted. He had done cases like this in the past with positive outcomes. I know Amir; if we were both responsible for repayment, the burden would all fall on me. That's why I fought so hard to get the IRS to separate the liability.

What I experienced at the hearing was baffling to my accountant, who had represented businesses and individuals at various income levels, from Fortune 500 companies to individuals like me trying to rebuild my financial situation. During my session with the IRS, I explained my situation, and I answered all the questions presented to me by the agent. When it was over, he looked at me and told me that he didn't care. He said it's not his problem that my ex-husband was not a nice guy and he wouldn't bother to go after him when he could get the money from me. I could tell that my accountant, who was sitting beside me, was shocked by what he was hearing. He began speaking on my behalf, explaining that I lost my home to foreclosure, had to file bankruptcy, and was working hard to support my two small children and my mom who lived with me. To that, he replied, "You're young and in a good job, so you can repay the loan." My accountant inquired as to whether, if I were making only $50,000 per year under the same circumstances, I could have been granted my request, to which he answered, "Absolutely, but she's not making $50,000, so this appeal is denied." I wanted to burst into tears, but I kept it together as best as I could.

On our car ride from Washington, D.C., back to my accountant's office in Montgomery County, he expressed how shocked he was not just by the outcome but also by the callous way in which the IRS representative treated me. I'm not one to always pull the race card and believe that everything negative that happens to me has to do with my race. But the more I listened to my Caucasian accountant express his surprise by my outcome, given that he had done this same thing before, I couldn't help but wonder. My Caucasian IRS petition officer did not see me or my situation. All he saw was a Black woman in a good job asking for "a favor" from the government. This, ladies, is called, "systemic racism" at its finest. I was not asking to be excused from paying the government back. I was asking for justice. This upwardly mobile Black woman was not asking the government for a handout. I worked hard every day to take care of my children, so it was unbelievable that I was penalized for working hard and getting rewarded at my job for that hard work.

I set up a repayment plan with the IRS where they withdrew money from my account monthly. I knew there would always be interest on that money until it was paid off in full. What I didn't know was that even with a repayment plan that I paid faithfully, there would be an additional penalty levied on the account each year. It took me several years to pay back half of the money. Then something amazing happened, and that's just how God works. Godmom suggested that I could take a loan from her, pay off the IRS, and then I could pay her back interest-free at my own pace. That was the best thing that could happen to me with this situation.

I ended up paying back the entire loan to the IRS, and as I suspected, Amir contributed nothing and did not have a repayment plan with the IRS. I called them numerous times, inquiring why they weren't going after him, but I couldn't get a satisfactory answer. It wasn't until one nice lady told me that as long as they were getting the money from me, the only thing the IRS would do was to hold any tax refund that Amir might get back. My only option would be to go after Amir in court to get him to pay me back his half. In addition to the IRS debt, there was $5,600 owed to the State of Maryland, and of that amount, I ended up paying $5,155. Ladies, this was a costly mistake, and the moral of this experience is that it's important for married women to understand that they are equally responsible in the sight of the IRS. It's important when filing a joint return to review the return carefully and not leave it all up to your husband.

God is good, all the time. I didn't have to wait long to experience His mercies and blessings. Five months after my ordeal started, I received some amazing news that would propel my career forward. I was working on the high-profile project for several months, and I was burning the midnight oil both in and out of the United States with monthly trips to London. I was approached for a position at the next level above me. I was surprised. I had only been in the company for two years, but I received a promotion just the year before and now was looking at another career jump. I had no doubt in my mind that the work I produced on this high-profile project was the catalyst for this career advancement. The icing on the cake came when I received my performance review from my manager that year. I couldn't believe that my bonus was four times the amount I received the prior year. I was speechless. It couldn't have come at a better time. The bonus, along with the new position and the pay increase, set me on the right footing to rebuild the financial future for my children and me.

Although money was tight because I was managing everything alone, I decided to use some of my bonus money for a family vacation. We spent three weeks in Jamaica, and it was exactly what we all needed. We spent two weeks at Mom's house in Kingston and one week at an all-inclusive resort in Ocho Rios. One of my besties, Shika, came to Jamaica to accompany me and the boys to the resort. It was great to see the children relax in a place that was different from their day-to-day environment. It was not an easy transition, especially for my oldest son. I had him in counseling with a child psychologist who was helping him with how he was feeling. Sometimes it was hard for me to sit and hear my five-year-old explain how much he missed his dad. It tore me apart when he shared how he felt whenever his dad made a promise to do something with him and he didn't show up. This was my new reality. But there was something about being on a tropical island, where it's easier to forget about my realities. The children were care-free, Shika and I caught up with each other's lives, and most importantly, I had the chance to thank my friend who was a tower of strength to me during my times of crisis.

June 28, 2010

It's resort time! Today we began our 5-night trip to Jamaica Grande Hotel in Ocho Rios. We are so excited to go and have some fun in the sun. We were supposed to leave earlier, but Mr. George (my Mom's husband) had to go to work, so we ended up getting to the resort around 9:30 p.m. We checked in and went straight to dinner. The boys were exhausted from the 2-hour ride to the hotel. We walked around the property a bit, went up to our room, and called it a night. We were all pretty beat. Once we got the boys settled into bed, Shika and I spent the next couple of hours catching up with each other's lives. Even though we haven't seen each other in two years, not a day goes by that we don't talk to each other, so we stay in pretty close contact. It is good to have a friend who has my back, no matter what. Shika is the type of girlfriend who will drop what she is doing to help. She knew that I needed this get-away, and I couldn't have done it by myself with the boys, so she volunteered to come on vacation with us. This is not the first time that she has done this. She is, indeed, my girl.

I had a lot of time to think while I was in Jamaica. Something about my homeland was therapeutic for me. Although my life was in turmoil, enjoying the beautiful sunshine, the white sandy beaches with crystal-clear water, and the delicious Jamaican meals somehow helped me to put things in perspective. Yes, I had setbacks, but I also achieved a lot at that time, and being in Jamaica brought a lot of those feelings to the forefront of my mind. I made plans for my life, and one of those long-term goals was to buy a home for me and my family.

I mapped out my financial situation, listing my short and long-term goals. I cut back on things that were not necessary, and I saved. I put every bonus I received from my job into an account that I called my "house account." We had basic cable and started taking local vacations. For vacation, I drove the family to Virginia for the week. It wasn't Jamaica, and the boys were not happy because they missed going to Jamaica, but children are resilient and will adapt to anything. I wanted to save money for my down payment, as well as furniture and necessities to outfit the home. When you have a foreclosure, there are rules that must be followed before you can obtain another loan for a home purchase. Three years after my foreclosure, I was able to purchase a home for my family. My focus and dedication paid off, and I did it all by myself! This was a major accomplishment for me because when I was going through my turmoil, I never saw this day. Let me correct myself: I was able to buy a house because the Lord Jesus made the provisions for me, for my situation was not too much for him. God is truly able.

March 9, 2013

Sidoney Samuels-Buckridge   **197**

Today I bought a house. Yeah!!! I'm so excited right now. This is my second time at Ryan Homes and even though the lender told me that I can't obtain a loan until after April 30th I decided to take my chances since this is a new home, and it will take them a while to build. It was sold before and fell through. They are offering over $50k in options to seal the deal. My home will be a mirror of the model home. I'm happy that they are finishing the basement. I gave them a check for $60,000 and looked around what will be my new home. The expected delivery is July, so we will go month-to-month for one month since my lease ends in June. I'm really happy about this.

August 22, 2013

Today is liberation day for me! After three years and eight months, I am finally able to settle and move into a beautiful home for my family, and as I sat at settlement, the realization that I did not let my ex-husband keep me down was a powerful feeling—I did it! Through discipline, savings, and a determination to get back on my feet, I was able to purchase a 4,000 plus square feet; $617,000 house all by myself. I know that I have to thank God because He is utterly amazing because I couldn't have done any of this without His help. I'm just so grateful. The boys were in awe when they saw their new home. Their excitement was contagious. This is what it's about!

Life Lessons From This Chapter:

- When life goes down, the only place you can go is up—take it one step at a time to rebuild your life.

- Fight for what is important during a divorce—for me, full custody of my children was non-negotiable.

- Don't mess with the IRS—these people are no joke. Pay attention to your taxes.

- Starting over is not easy—sometimes leaving a toxic situation is the best thing for your life.

- The Lord will make a way where there seems to be no way.

CHAPTER 6

I AM SO DONE, GOD!

"Now unto him that is able to do exceeding abundantly above all that we ask or think, according to the power that worketh in us."

—Ephesians 3:20 (KJV)

Starting over was not easy. A 35-year-old single mom was not what I envisioned for myself in all my life planning. I lost myself in my marriage, and it was evident that I had to find out who I was at that juncture in my life. I knew I had the ability to be the provider for my family, and I did that. I spent a considerable amount of time focused on rebuilding our lives, but at the same time, it was important for me to take a hard look at myself, evaluate where I was, where I wanted to be, and take the steps necessary to love myself again. I knew that I needed to rediscover myself and work on "me." I would be no good to anyone else—my children, Mom, or a future partner—if I didn't. I spent that first year getting myself better physically, spiritually, and emotionally.

The marriage took a toll on my body. I used to be at a healthy weight at several points in my life. There is no magic to this. I knew what I needed to do to lose weight: eat a balanced diet and exercise. Stress, eating, and a lack of time devoted to exercise packed on the pounds over the years. When I left Amir, I topped the scale at my highest at 200 pounds. This was not ideal for my 5-foot-4-inch frame. I did some soul searching because I was determined to get Sidoney back. I had some trouble carving out time for myself. I was so accustomed to being everything to everyone that to incorporate diet and exercise into my life, I had to schedule it on my calendar. I had a lot to fix in my life to truly start living again. I was angry at God because of what happened to me, I was bitter towards men, and I was convinced that my fate was to remain by myself.

When I left Amir, I moved to a house five miles from my job. The close proximity to work gave me back two hours of my day that was used for commuting. That allowed me more time for myself. I repurposed my commute time to my exercise time. I cleaned up my diet and resorted to a lower-carb diet, made up of mostly meat and vegetables. The pounds started melting off. I dropped Amir and the 50 extra pounds I was carrying around. It felt great to get back into my size-10 clothing. I had been that size five years prior. It took me a year to accomplish that goal. I was happy that I learned different techniques to manage my stress, which is always going to be a part of life. Instead of relying on food for comfort, I found myself exercising, walking, or reading a book. I took the time to figure out who I was and what habits I wanted to adopt in my "new life."

As I began to feel better, I noticed that my Crohn's disease, for the most part, remained in remission and was being managed by drug therapy, and no steroids like in years past. Achieving work/life satisfaction was one area that I struggled with. The few times I had flareups, it was linked to a stressful situation either in my personal or professional life. My work stresses were the usual—handling the challenges of being a woman of color trying to survive in Corporate America. Those stresses seemed to follow me to every job I went to. These included inequalities, unrealistic expectations for women of color, and lack of sponsors to help me advance. These challenges were on top of being a working single mother. These realities will never change, and my constant struggle was to figure out coping mechanisms.

Ladies, I know this is no surprise to you; especially if you're a single mom, you know what I'm talking about. Those who are married also have similar challenges because it's usually the woman who handles most, if not all, of the tasks associated with running a household on top of holding down full-time jobs. It became a juggling act for me. Being a single mom with little to no help from the other parent required careful planning and trade-offs, and some weeks were better than others. There was no manual that I could flip that would give me the answers. There was no formula. What I found that worked for me was to cut myself some slack. I was not a superwoman, and sometimes I got things wrong because of pure exhaustion. I had to learn to be happy with 80 percent effort, which wasn't easy for me because I always strive to do my best. I began learning that sometimes my best was not 100 percent, and I had to live with this reality.

September 6, 2011

I'm boarding a plane right now heading to London for a business trip. I worked a 10-hour day today, and now I am truly exhausted. My goal is to just eat the meal they offer and try and get a good night's sleep and be prepared to work some long hours for the rest of the week. I dropped Emilien off at school today, and he had a smile on his face. I hope he continues to enjoy school for the rest of the year. I was able to do homework with the boys and get them settled before I took off for my trip. It's so difficult for me every time I have to leave my boys. I know that my Mom will take the absolute best care of them, but still, I'm not at home doing the home-work or helping with the nighttime ritual. I will never get accustomed to leaving them, but I have a remarkably high travel volume in the next couple of weeks.

My job at the time was very demanding and required a signifi-cant amount of business travel. The first year I left Amir, I was traveling once per month to London and each trip was one-week long. Because I was responsible for 95 percent of the children's care, I was lucky to have my mom living with me to help ease the burden. However, there were things that she could not help with. Transporting the boys to their numerous activities—piano lessons, track, basketball—fell on me. Help-ing with homework and maneuvering the new public school system was also on me. A big chunk of my time was spent helping my oldest through the transition of being separated from his dad. There were many setbacks, therapy sessions, and meltdowns.

Sometimes it required being up at 2 a.m. with a child and getting up and being in the office at 7 a.m., operating on little sleep but carefully applying makeup to hide the tired look that I knew was on my face. I worried about my children that being raised in two different households would have a negative impact on their lives. I had to pick up the pieces when their dad disappointed them and didn't show up after he promised he would. I was a hands-on parent, but at times I wished Amir would do his part. The reality of my situation was that repeatedly I was being both mom and dad. Amir was bitter, and the simplest thing that I asked him to do for the boys was met with a response like "You wanted full custody, so deal with it." I guess he had forgotten that these were also his children. The only card he had was the children. Initially, I would react when he showed up late to pick up the kids or when he brought them back late at night without giving them a shower or feeding them. I quickly realized that he was trying to get under my skin to get me worked up. I eventually changed my reaction to no reaction, and it became bearable. These were new territories that I was dealing with. To move on, I had to get Amir out of my head. We were no longer together, so he should not be allowed to interfere with my life, and I was the only one who could make that happen.

My conscious decision to forego dating for one year post my departure from Amir was the best decision I made. Emotionally, I was in no shape to pursue any type of relationship. With all my life experiences, I wanted to ensure that the second time around, I did everything in my power to make better choices with whom I chose to date and subsequently pursue a relationship. Dating this time would be different because now in the equation I had two children and a mom who were part of my package. I was looking for a family-oriented, God-fearing man, and I would not settle for less because I was in no rush.

One of my 2011 resolutions was to start dating. I had been off the market for 15 years when I decided to venture out into the dating world. Who was I kidding? I was out of my element, and I got solicited and unsolicited advice from many. The common theme I heard was that dating was different and online dating was the way to go. I was hesitant at first to put my personal information into an online dating platform. I eventually took the plunge and paid for my first three months with a popular dating site. It felt like a job interview. I had to answer a million questions, do a compatibility test so that the system could provide me with the most appropriate matches, and most importantly, I had to create the most appealing profile with the right photos so that it stood out to get that much-anticipated match. One weekend, I waited until the boys were with Amir to get started on this task that I was not looking forward to. I pushed ahead, got through the set-up stage, and then I waited and waited.

I wasn't sure if online dating was for me. I'm more of an old-fashioned type when it comes to dating. Why couldn't I meet someone and we start up a conversation that could lead to a successful date? When I brought up these points to my online dating "experts" who were recommending this path, they asked me the one magic question: "Where are you going to meet men?" That question stopped me in my tracks. They were right—because the only places I went to were work, church, and the grocery store. I didn't want to mix my work and personal life, so dating someone at work was out. That left church and the grocery store. I went to church once a week, and the grocery store once every two weeks. The odds of meeting someone was grim with those probabilities. I asked God to guide me because I was scared to make another relationship mistake.

The profiles came in and the instruction was to reach out to profiles you found interesting and start a conversation. The first month, I did nothing. After all, in my head, *Women are not supposed to chase men. The men who are interested should reach out.* And they did. I began corresponding with Michael, a charmer, originally from Nigeria who had one story after another. Quickly, I realized that with online dating, people could hide behind a computer and a series of texts and you'd never really know exactly who you were dealing with. I quickly ended my correspondence with Michael after he asked me for money. Who asks someone for money whom they haven't even met? My guard was up, and I was alert. There were a few others who reached out, and I had brief connections with them.

After three months of the dating site taking my monthly payment, and I was not receiving matches that I thought were appropriate, I quit that one and signed up with another. The second time was easier because I copied my profile and began the same process all over again on the new dating platform. A European man reached out to me right away. We corresponded through the site and shortly thereafter exchanged phone numbers. We spoke for a few weeks on the phone before our first date. What I didn't know then was the impact this man would have on my life. I do believe that everyone comes into your life for a reason and a season.

I knew right away that Juan was different from the others. He was honest with me from the onset, which is a rarity with online dating. He was a foreign assignee from Spain, working in the government as a scientist. When I met him, I initially thought that I shouldn't pursue a relationship with him because he wouldn't be in the U.S. for a long time and, in fact, had only six months left in the country. I thought, *Why waste my time?* As I got to know Juan, I threw caution to the wind and decided to date him and just enjoy the time we had together. After all, I wasn't trying to marry him. In fact, at that time in my life, I had no intention of marrying anyone again. Juan was a couple of "firsts" for me: He was the first man whom I dated after I left Amir, he was the first Caucasian man I dated, and he was my first European partner. Juan's season in my life was to expose me to what it should be like when you have someone in your life who really cares about you. For the number of years I was with Amir, you would think that I would be all caught up and couldn't learn anything new from a partner.

The opposite happened to me. I was learning what it felt like to be in a healthy relationship. I was not scared to show and receive affection, I was having deep conversations, and I was learning how to resolve conflicts. I told myself not to fall for Juan because he would leave the U.S. and I would be heart-broken. The heart is funny though. You can tell it one thing, and it does the complete opposite. I fell for Juan. What was there not to fall for? He was caring, generous, and treated me well. I love Black men and only dated Black men up to that time. I will say that color doesn't define a person, and people are unique individuals. I was with a Black man whom many would describe as the perfect exterior package—dark, handsome, with a great body. However, he brought me nothing but pain. It took a Caucasian man to show me how I should be treated as a woman. I would have never had this opportunity if I had closed off my mind and declared that I would only date Black men. Juan's color never bothered me because I got to know him as a person, and in my mind, that is most important. We all know how it is in the United States; we still have people who are bigots. We got stares, but I never let other people's opinions and rudeness bother me. I was having the time of my life. I was enjoying dinners, dancing, hanging out, talking, you name it. I was having fun. Ladies, you know what I'm talking about. Sometimes, no matter what you tell your heart, it just doesn't cooperate!

July 9, 2011

I spent the night at Juan's place, and I got up this morning and made him a nice breakfast—eggs, bacon, and toast with a glass of orange juice. It's nice to cook for a man and to see him enjoy it. It's been a while. It's good to just lounge around with a man who tells you constantly how beautiful you are. This is my new reality, and I have to pinch myself to ask whether this is really happening or not. After my split with Amir, I never thought I would ever meet someone decent. Juan is a nice guy, who treats me like a queen. It's a shame that at the end of next month he will be going back to Spain. Juan and I hung out at the pool for the better part of the day. We laid out getting some rays, relaxing, and reading. We had an early dinner at a nice Italian restaurant where they cook the meal right in front of you. A day well spent. It's nice to be in someone's arms. A sister could get accustomed to this type of life.

At the end of August 2011, Juan boarded a plane. My six-months of dating, being pampered, and living again came to an end. As much as I tried not to get attached, it happened anyway. My plan just to enjoy the time we had while Juan was in the U.S. also did not go as planned. Juan and I found ourselves in a long-distance relationship. Skype, texting, and phone calls became our ways of communicating. While not ideal, we tried to make it work. It was somewhat manageable because I was in Europe frequently for work, so Juan and I were able to connect during those visits. I didn't know how long this arrangement would last, but we continued. It was tough not having him around when I was dealing with challenges, and I knew he was beginning to get lonely. A month after his departure, I had my first visit to Madrid, Spain. I had a five-day stay after a two-week trip to Europe for work. I met Juan's family and visited many tourist sites. I enjoyed the siesta. Juan showed me around his hometown. It was as if we picked up right where we left off. I loved the casual atmosphere in Madrid, including an afternoon glass of wine at one of the sidewalk cafes and meeting Juan's friends for nibbles. It was difficult to say goodbye, but in two months, Juan was taking me to Mexico for a week to celebrate my 37th birthday, so I had something to look forward to.

I had the time of my life in Mexico. Juan and I had much to celebrate. We were celebrating my birthday and my new job. It felt so good to be carefree and not worry about taking care of the kids, meeting work deadlines, or arguing with Amir. It was an unforgettable birthday, and Juan planned everything to the last detail. He even brought the "37" number candles to put in my cake that he arranged with the restaurant. I never had a man take me on an overseas vacation before where he covered the cost. It was nice. After our trip to Mexico, we headed back to the U.S. where Juan spent three more days with me before returning to Spain.

We finally got up and dressed at around 10 a.m. We went to the mall and shared a cup of Starbucks before shopping for some clothes for Juan. He got some really good deals. We went home to have lunch and at 12:30 p.m., we headed to the airport. It was a solemn ride for both of us. Juan kept holding my hand and kissing it. The elephant in the room is that both of us are so torn that we will have to leave each other without knowing exactly when we will see each other again. Juan and I shared hugs and passionate kisses before he grabbed his luggage to get into the airport. Luckily, I brought him to the airport early because he barely made it to his flight. I needed to do something with myself to take my mind off him, so I went shopping. It was so hard for me to fall asleep. I miss Juan. Gosh, I'm really sad right now.

When Juan boarded the plane back to Spain, my head was telling me that I needed to move on and start dating again so I could find a man who lived on the same continent. However, my heart was screaming no—I wanted that man in Spain. When I sat down to do my 2012 resolutions, one was "to get back on the dating scene." Juan and I talked about that, and we both agreed to start dating other people. It was hard, and I didn't know if I would find someone like this man again. After a year of not being on a dating site, I signed up once more, hoping that I would get lucky again like I did with Juan. An interesting thing happened: All the matches that I got and the men whom I spoke to just did not add up to what I had become accustomed to with Juan. In a nutshell, I was spoiled. With my new dating experience, I now had standards that I expected the men I was dating to meet. Ladies, it's particularly important to have standards. Know what you want and wait until you get that person in your life. Don't allow family or friends to tell you that you are too "picky." Knowing your worth means that you won't accept mediocracy from the men you date. Juan and I continued to communicate, but it was different. We were becoming more like friends. In April 2012, I was in Europe for work, and I made a trip to Spain to see Juan. That was the last time we saw each other.

April 29, 2012

I'm on a plane heading home. I spent the weekend in Madrid with Juan. I had a really good time like I always do with Juan. This time was a bit different. It's the closure I needed to move on and make myself available to welcome new interests in my life and to really start dating again. Juan has met someone, and we talked about it. I needed to do this face-to-face. I experienced a sadness that I didn't feel when Amir and I split where I felt a sense of loss. I knew this day was coming, but reality is difficult. I know that Juan and I will always be friends, for we have developed a really good friendship where we are there for each other. However, I have to move on to ensure that I'm not a fallback person if this relationship does not work out for him. I will have to move on, and I will forever cherish what I had with him.

Juan was in my life for a reason and a season. It was a great season. I learned a lot about myself, and my self-esteem improved. He renewed my faith in men. I realized that I shouldn't allow my experience with Amir to dissuade me from pursuing another relationship. When I was with Juan, I was happy. I smiled a lot. I was giddy as a teenager, and it felt good. I was now in a better position to re-enter the dating world. This time I had a clearer picture of what I was looking for—a God-fearing and honest man who would cherish and treat me well. Could I find that again through online dating?

Juan and I have remained friends who share in each other's joys and sorrows. Who knew we would be in each other's lives for ten years? After Juan, I was on the dating rollercoaster for six years before my situation changed. There were a few highs but mostly lows. There were some funny situations, some unbelievable experiences, and I was growing tired of online dating. I changed various dating platforms over the years, but the experience was all the same, regardless of whichever online dating site I signed up with. On a plane ride from London, I was reading the inflight magazine and found an intriguing article about a dating service that catered to the busy professional. What I found appealing was that it appeared they did most of the work and all the client had to do was say yes to a match and go out on the dates. I thought that was the answer to my dating woes, something exclusive. I got online and researched if there was one local to my area, and sure enough, there was.

I reached out, and this was different. It cost five times what you would pay for a typical online dating service. I had to go in for an interview; they took their own photos and built a profile for me. They sent me matches and I had to determine the ones I was interested in, then they set up the dates. I thought this was the answer, but what I learned was that this was just an overpriced online dating service. It was the same as the others; it just cost more. In the beginning, some of the men I was matched with seemed great, but there had to be mutual interest in meeting for it to be a compatible connection. When I complained, they told me the men that were interested in me were not the ones that I showed interest in. I wasn't getting dates set up because it's based on compatibility. I tried to get my money back after one year passed without getting a date. They said that wasn't possible because my contract stipulated that they would provide me with 10 dates, which, however, they didn't have to do so in a given time period. I couldn't get my money back because there was no expiration date for the program—basically another rip-off. In fact, over the course of six years, I received one date from the so-called exclusive dating service. While I had this service, I also kept one of the typical online dating services. I even complained to my "exclusive" dating service that I had more success with the other traditional online dating service that didn't cost half as much as I paid them, but that didn't do anything.

I went on many first dates, and there was never a second date, by choice. I became an expert at weeding through the lies on the first date and ended things. It became exhausting at times, so I took several breaks along the way. I would put my online dating account on a three-month break, or I would quit one altogether for six months before signing up with a new dating platform. This became my pattern.

I was dating, but nothing was materializing. I was determined, however, not to lower my standards for what I was looking for. Many women have a list of who they are looking for while dating. Initially, when I started dating, I didn't have a list, per se, but I wanted a man with a professional career. Amir and I were at different places in our careers and that was a bone of contention between us. Juan was a scientist and things clicked for us. In my flawed thinking, I thought that a man with a professional career would be a better fit because he would understand the pressures of my career versus a man who didn't.

So, I did go out on dates with professional men, and boy, was my theory flawed. I dated a doctor, a businessman, another scientist, and an FBI agent, just to name a few. I was sharing my philosophy with my friend Vince, and he rightfully informed me that I have cut out a large segment of men whom I wouldn't give a chance just because of the work that they did. I didn't look at it from that perspective. He asked me what I wanted, and I told him I wanted a God-fearing man who would treat me well. He challenged me to be more open and to look at each person as an individual.

I was ready to try Vince's suggestion because my track record with the professional men wasn't a good one. I have some interesting stories and dating woes that would have you laughing and shaking your head. I dated a doctor who had a problem with my work hours. He only saw patients from 9 a.m. to 3 p.m. and he complained that I didn't have enough time for him. I thought we had a lot in common because he was a single dad raising two children close in age with my children. Basically, in his eyes, because he was a doctor, his job was more important than mine, and I needed to alter my schedule to accommodate his. A funny thing happened with him.

One weekend, we had a date planned and he kept complaining about how dirty his house was. I had never been to his house, so I had no idea what it looked like. He kept talking about it, but I guess I was slow and was not catching on what he was leading to. To my horror, he came right out and asked me if I would clean his house after our date. I told him that I would not be cleaning his house, and I recommended he hire a cleaner. I was happy to let him know that things wouldn't work out between us. This man was a doctor, and he wouldn't pay to get his house cleaned!

Mr. FBI agent was fine with me having children, but he insisted that a stipulation for dating me was that his needs had to always come before the children's. After the first date, that was a goodbye from me. Mr. Businessman was a D.C. area socialite who supposedly lost all his wealth due to his divorce. His wife who was a doctor, according to him, got everything in the divorce, and he was at the time renting a basement. What did he want from me? He wanted me to work with him until he got on his feet, and in addition, he wanted me to spot him money to cover our date. Ladies, if a man can't afford to pay for a meal, then he should not be trying to date you. I know some people will not agree with me but hear me out. I believe that if you ask someone out on a date, it is your responsibility to cover the cost of the date. If there are subsequent dates, then I'm all for the woman chipping in to cover the cost.

The funniest story of all was a date I had with a "Christian" professional man whom I thought shared the same Christian values I had. What transpired on the first date was comic relief. He sent me photos of himself that had to have been taken 20 years prior. When I showed up at the restaurant for lunch, the man who greeted me was older and his belly was hanging over his belt. He looked like he was 50 pounds heavier than in the photos he sent me. That wasn't even the funniest part. In our conversations, we talked a lot about our faith and how important it was to us.

At the restaurant, we made small talk until our meals arrived. I ordered a salad, and he ordered a full meal. I was trying my best to get through the meal. When the waitress brought our food, my date grabbed my hand and started praying so loudly that I feared the whole restaurant could hear him. He was praying for a long time. I opened my eyes and saw couples to my right and left laughing. I wish I could disappear. He was oblivious, and once he stopped praying, he tore into his meal and finished it in no time. I was barely eating my salad when he asked if I was going to eat that, meaning he wanted the salad too. I told him to go ahead and help himself to my salad, which he gladly did.

To top it off, my "Christian" date spent the whole time oversharing about his ex-wife. He spent the majority of the time talking about the many things she did wrong. To make matters worse, he wanted to show me inappropriate photos of her on his phone that he discovered she was sending to another man. Why this man wanted to share this with me, I had no idea, so I politely declined. When he finished polishing off my salad and paid the bill, I couldn't get out of the restaurant fast enough. When he asked for a second date, I told him, "I think not!" Today, I can laugh at that dating disaster, but when I was going through it, I was mortified.

I was exhausted and disappointed with online dating. I was tired of meeting one "Mr. Wrong" after another, so I quit all the online dating sites and decided that I couldn't be bothered with dating anymore. I had enough, so I became content with being by myself, and with my track record, I didn't think I would ever find someone with whom I wanted to pursue a relationship.

Life Lessons From This Chapter:

- After leaving a toxic relationship, spend the time to rebuild yourself—mentally, physically, and spiritually.

- Schedule "me" time—doing everything for everyone while neglecting yourself is not the answer.

- Young children regress after a traumatic episode like a divorce—ensure you provide the appropriate help for your children.

- Ask for help—single motherhood with a full-time demanding job can break you.

- Even when I was angry at God, He was merciful towards me.

CHAPTER 7

TRANSFORMATION— WITH GOD ALL THINGS ARE POSSIBLE!

Jesus looked at them and said, "With man this is impossible, but with God all things are possible."

—Matthew 19:26 (KJV)

They say when you least expect it, the right person will come into your life. I was on a break from dating when I was introduced to the man who became my second chance at love. Initially, I was very skeptical that it would ever happen—where was my faith? For years after my world turned upside down, the Lord and I had a strained relationship. I went to church on Sundays and I prayed, but I wouldn't call what I had with the Lord a relationship. I put Him on the back burner while I did my own thing. I went to Him periodically, but a personal relationship with Him was absent as I wrestled with my faith. Truth be told, it was always one-sided, because while I was angry with God, He never gave up on me. At this stage in my life, I finally did what I should have done a long time ago, as instructed in 1 Peter 5:7 "Casting all your care upon him; for he cares for you." When I did, it all became abundantly clear. In the past, I prayed for a man of God to be part of my life. After eight years when there was no man or a prospect of one, I gave up. There is a saying that the Lord works in His time and not ours, and that was exactly what happened to me.

On April 21, 2018, on a day when I was looking my worst—think sweatpants, ponytail, and no makeup—a mutual friend introduced me to the man who would become my husband. His name is Renson. He didn't waste time and called me later that same evening we met, and we chatted and started to get to know each other. Renson and I share some similarities: We are both Jamaicans, we love the beach, and we love fine dining. We have some differences as well: He is a chef, and his career is different from mine. Luckily, at the time of our meeting, I was a much different person than the one who started on my dating journey. Had I not changed, I would not have been open to dating a person who had something other than a white-collar career. I evolved as a dater, and in my opinion, that evolution helped me to look at him as an individual. When we met, I had no expectations. I thought, *Why not?* That was the first time I was introduced to someone. A first date followed a week later. As a serial first dater, I always approached the first date like a reporter's interview—"the 5 W's and the H." In my mind, the first date is where I have the opportunity to learn the Who, What, When, Where, Why, and How. The men who failed never got a second date.

I was intrigued by Renson because he wasn't telling me what I wanted to hear. He even challenged me on that first date. And while I was taken aback, it caused me to want to learn more. On our first date, Renson asked me what I thought about marriage. For me, that was a loaded question, one I wasn't expecting on a first date, so I wasn't as prepared for an answer. I told him I didn't believe that marriage was in the cards for me. I further explained that I didn't see myself getting married again after what I went through with my ex-husband.

Renson, who had also been married and divorced, did not share the same outlook. He told me that even though he had been divorced, he was a family guy who believed in marriage. Initially, I was a bit taken aback because I thought he was a little cocky. I knew for sure this was going nowhere because I wasn't marrying anyone. While I thought that, his response left me wanting to learn more. So, when he asked for a second date on the spot, I agreed. I never agreed to a second date on the spot, even if I liked my date. I always explained that I needed to check my calendar and will get back to them. There was something different about this man, and I wanted to learn more.

I knew he was a man worth dating, especially when he did not balk when I told him about my "90-Day Rule." Like many women, I've read Steve Harvey's book *Act Like a Lady, Think Like a Man.* His points about waiting at least 90 days before being intimate with a man you're dating resonated with me, and I decided I'd stick to that rule. Steve points out that women need time to carefully evaluate if the situation is right for them and that sexual intercourse frequently clouds judgment. To no surprise, an interesting thing happened to me repeatedly during previous dates: The minute I mentioned my "90-day" rule, that would be the end of whatever was developing. That was fine with me because I wanted someone who wanted to get to know me and who wasn't just interested in my "goods." When I mentioned my 90-Day Rule to Renson, his response was "That is fine and it works for me because that's not why I'm with you." I knew this man was a keeper because I had never received that response before, and it was a breath of fresh air. We could focus on the task of getting to know each other without this added pressure. I found myself falling for Renson more quickly than I had for anyone else.

I refused to admit this to him or anyone else because I was scared. I began praying. I found myself talking to God and asking him what was happening. It's also interesting how the people in your life can see what you are not able to see. Of course, I shared my experience with my two besties, Shika and Jackie. They had been around for my highs and lows. They had heard all my dating drama, and sometimes we laughed. They were the ones who got me through some of my dating disasters. Interestingly, Shika became my "escape." Whenever I was on a date that was a disaster, I would politely excuse myself to the restroom to call her, asking for her to rescue me with a phone call when I got back to the date. Jackie kept urging me to keep praying and not to give up on men, especially our Black men, when I was experiencing some trying times. It was no surprise to my besties that something was different this time around, especially when I began talking to them about introducing Renson to the boys.

Around the three-month mark, I introduced him to the boys and Mom. In the nine years that I was dating, this was only the second time that I brought a man around my mom and children. The last time was eight years prior when I was with Juan, and the boys were four and seven years old then. I didn't know what to expect from my tween and teenager, but I took a chance. My youngest, Emilien, who had been begging for a stepdad for years was won over first. My oldest, Sebastien, had a wait-and-see approach.

June 19, 2018

Today is Renson's time to spend with the boys. He's been getting closer to them as he comes to their track practices. I had to take Mommy to a doctor's appointment so Renson picked them up from Vacation Bible School and took them to BGR for a burger and then they went to the movies. The boys had a good time, especially Emilien. I believe he has won Emilien over with this gesture. I'm feeling happy myself as he begins to win me over. He's so sweet and thoughtful. I enjoy the dates and getting to know him. Most of all, I enjoy the small things he does for me, getting me a cell phone case, picking up the boys when I can't. I'm hoping that this relationship works out for us. I'm going to take it slow and get to know him. I like that Renson is a family and God-fearing guy. As a Christian, it makes a difference. I'm praying that we can work together to make this work. I know it won't be easy because I'm so scared of relationships and to make myself vulnerable, but I want to be with someone and that's the chance I will have to make.

I remember a conversation that Renson and I had around the three-month mark. We went out to dinner and I was explaining to him that I was surprised that he had lasted as long as he did. In retrospect, I'm not sure if I needed to have this conversation to put the protective veil around my heart or whether this was my way of sabotaging the relationship. Renson was never deterred by my attempts to push him away. Initially, I didn't see the possibility of a long-term relationship, but the more I was around him, the more I wasn't sure exactly what I wanted anymore. Somehow, we got on the topic of marriage again, and Renson asked me how I felt about marriage. He further went on to talk about what God's plan is for couples in relationships. I was still not convinced that marriage was in the cards for me, so I answered from my heart. Renson was the first one to use the "L" word. When he told me that he loved me the first time, I froze! Ladies, I know that some of you know what I'm talking about here. Honestly, I didn't know what to say because my heart was beating a mile a minute. I didn't say anything because I was scared of what would come out of my mouth. I wanted to tell him I loved him also, but I didn't want to think about what that response would lead to, so I said nothing.

Saying nothing is never a good response, but I am fortunate that I had a man who was patient with me. I was very transparent with Renson about my journey and experience with Amir. I needed him to understand my realities so he would have a better sense of where my thinking was. It was no surprise to me when early on Renson told me that I put up a wall. Yes, I had a wall around my heart because I didn't want another man to hurt me nor did I want any drama in my life. I was scared to take a leap of faith. But Renson kept making me laugh, making me feel special. Day by day, he began chipping away at the wall that I had built around my heart.

I began to fall in love with Renson. I didn't want to be away from him for long periods, I looked forward to his texts and phone calls, and the more time we spent together, I began to realize that whatever was happening between us felt right. I felt comfortable sharing various aspects of my life with him. We talked about my goals, future plans, and fears. He's a greater listener and offered a different perspective. I loved our discussions about any and everything, especially when he got fired up about his faith. The passion he had for God was exactly what I was looking for in a partner. Renson was so considerate of my needs, and he made it his duty to ensure that I was happy. Being happy in a relationship doesn't come easily to me, but Renson made it so effortless, and I found myself letting go of my fears and embracing this man.

August 2, 2018

Renson is back from Miami. I'm so glad to have my baby back with me. After my meeting, I picked him up from the restaurant down the street. I can tell that my baby missed me. It was a little different having him in the house with no one else there because my gang was in Jamaica. At first, it was a bit awkward, but that passed very quickly. I heated up some leftovers and gave him dinner. Watching us being together has me thinking if this is what it would look like if he became a permanent part of my life. It's interesting that since I left my ex-husband nine years ago, I've never met anyone whom

I would consider to be part of my life permanently. What is it about Renson? He is kind, patient, tender, and he loves me. He has used the "L" word and I finally reciprocated! It really scares me, but I'm beginning to fall in love with this man. Can this happen so soon? I feel like I've known him forever. He listens to me, and he is into me. My head is screaming caution, but my heart is screaming to let go.

Renson and I began planning our first vacation together. He wanted us to go to Miami over Thanksgiving so that I could meet his family and his daughter who resided there. He wanted the people who meant the most to him to get to know me. I was nervous about this trip because I knew it meant a lot to Renson, and it seemed like our relationship was entering a serious phase. The closer we got to the vacation, the more nervous I got because at that time, if he were to propose, I wasn't sure what my answer would be.

I was wrestling with the feelings that I was having about Renson and the future direction of our relationship. I had no doubt what his feelings were for me. It wasn't his words but his actions towards me and how much he embraced the boys and my mom. I could no longer deny that he was now part of my life, and at the six-month mark, I got some invaluable advice from my mentor of 11 years. A mentoring relationship means that you not only share professional challenges but personal struggles as well. My mentor could see the positive changes that having Renson in my life was doing for me and the family. During our discussions, she always inquired about how the relationship was progressing.

I believe that a discussion I had with my mentor helped provide the clarity I needed to finally open my heart to the possibilities. My mentor was there during my tumultuous relationship with Amir, during the divorce, and she watched me rebuild a life for my family. In September 2018, we had a lighthearted talk about how well things were going in my relationship. Very quickly, the jovial conversation turned into a serious "mother-daughter" discussion. My mentor inquired, "So when is the wedding?" Of course, I thought she was joking, but she wasn't. I almost hyperventilated when she told me that if Renson proposed on our vacation, I'd better accept.

At first, I assured her that there was no way that would be taking place so soon, so I had nothing to worry about. My mentor knew me well. She could sense I was deflecting, and she did not allow me to get away with it. She pushed and helped me to acknowledge and address my fears. I walked away from that meeting in a daze. Her words kept ringing in my ears: *Are you going to allow fear to keep you from living? This is a good man; he loves you; he treats the boys and your mom well, and I've never seen you happier.* After that meeting, I began to seriously consider the possibilities. I'm not going to lie and say I had this miraculous awakening. I continued to wrestle with what I would do. I asked myself why I couldn't just be with him and not get married. After all, many people these days are perfectly fine with those types of relationships.

The glaring flaw with that thinking was that 'I'm not most people.' I know what God wanted me to do, and knowing Renson like I did, I knew that he would not go for an arrangement like that. The Lord was working on me, big time. There was no denying that I knew His word, and I knew the teachings, and I had my two sons to consider as well. I wanted to ensure that the behavior that I was displaying in front of them was becoming. Being in a long-term relationship with a man I was not married to was not the example I wanted to set for them. I had to deal with my internal struggles without involving Renson because I wanted clarity. And after all, he hasn't asked me to marry him.

The Lord never makes mistakes. He knows the desires of our heart, and He knows what's best for us, even when we don't. The Lord's timing is always perfect. I often wondered, *Why Renson?* You see, God had a plan that I wasn't privy to. When we met, Renson was on his own journey with his Christianity. He explained to me how he was once on fire for God, and he was no longer at that place. In essence, we were both at a crossroads in our faith. I grew up and got baptized in a Church of God, and I later moved to the Catholic Church. During the Catholic Church scandal, I left that faith and began attending a nondenominational church. Renson got saved in the Apostolic faith and was working on getting back to the place he needed to be with God. I knew in my heart that God was at work. Let me break it down for you. Mom had been attending an Apostolic Church for more than eight years while the boys and I attended our nondenominational church. She had invited me on numerous occasions to her church, and I politely declined.

My church service was one hour, and Mom's was close to two-hours long. Over the years, I became acquainted with some of her friends from church. They too invited me to attend, and I declined. What are the odds that now the man that I was dating was from the Apostolic faith and the same exact church? Is that a coincidence? Absolutely not. As Renson found his way back to his faith, we all started attending the Apostolic Church together—Renson, Mom, the boys, and I. What I loved about my new church was how diverse it was. There are cultures represented from all over the world.

As an immigrant, I fit right in because of the large immigrant population in the congregation. There were so many Caribbean, African, South American, and European immigrants. Culturally, I was at home, but I had to get accustomed to the longer services. Besides, the service was different from what I was used to; the way people dressed was different from what I knew. I grew up in church most of my life, and I found that I was now learning things I never knew. I went out and bought some dresses because at my nondenominational church I could wear whatever I wanted. I looked around at the new church, and only visitors were not in dresses or skirts. As time went on, I began to notice less and less how long the services were. I was, for the first time in a long time, feeling the presence of God in my life. I had no idea where any of this was going. I found myself searching for my Bible that was gathering dust on my bookshelf. I opened it up, and I started reading. Renson and I were engaging in more discussions about the Lord. I found myself asking him questions about the Apostolic faith. I challenged him about some of the teachings that I was learning. Our relationship was taking a turn. I found myself no longer worried about the future direction and all the fears I had.

Christmas is my favorite holiday. Celebrating Jesus' birth has significant meaning in my faith. I also enjoy this time of year, especially being with family and friends. It's a tradition of mine to take an extended time off from work while the boys are on Christmas break so that we could spend quality time together. This was Renson's first Christmas with my extended family, and he joined the merriment with laughter, games, and the traditional Jamaican Christmas meal—rice and peas, oxtail, jerk chicken, curried goat, sorrel, and black cake.

On December 25, 2018, I had another reason to celebrate; Renson proposed, and I accepted! Mom, the boys, my cousin, and brother with his family were all there to witness the occasion

December 25, 2018

It's Christmas Day. I'm blessed that I live to see another year to celebrate Jesus' birth. I was up early at 6 a.m. and went

downstairs at 7 a.m. where our family had a large Jamai-can breakfast. We had fried dumpling, ackee and saltfish, breadfruit, and fried plantains. I had a little bit of breakfast because I'm not feeling well. We opened gifts right after breakfast and the boys were in heaven. Emilien rolled in $325 and Sebastien $400. Dwayne showed up at 2 p.m. and we were all doting over Sasha. Dwayne and Monique opened their gifts, then we played a game of Taboo. Renson did the most beautiful thing, he asked me to marry him. He had a beautiful speech. He told me that since the first day he met me, my smile lit up his world. He said he was ready to spend the rest of his life to continue to make me happy and humbly asked if I would do him the honor and be his wife. He got down on his knees and presented me with a beautiful three-carat emerald cut diamond ring. My engagement ring is so beautiful. I feel special that he did the engagement in front of my family. This was one of my best Christmases. Thank you, God, for all my blessings.

Renson took a leap of faith when he asked me to marry him. I later learned that my mom and brother had been aware of it since Thanksgiving. Before we went on our vacation, Renson asked them for their blessing. I had been resistant to the idea of marriage in previous discussions, so he had no way of knowing what my answer would be when he asked my mom and brother. When we had the marriage discussion while on vacation, my mentor's words kept ringing in my ears, and this was the first time that my response was somewhat hopeful. I told him that I wasn't sure if marriage were for me right now, but I was beginning to think that it could be a possibility in the future. After Renson proposed, and he and I had a moment to ourselves, we began to talk. I was shocked when he told me that on that first day he met me, he knew that I would be his wife. I was not surprised to learn that Renson was praying for guidance from God about our relationship. Honestly, I never saw marriage in my future, but that's how my God works. He knows everything about me, and as he said in Jeremiah 1:5 *"Before I shaped you in the womb, I knew all about you. Before you saw the light of day, I had holy plans for you: A prophet to the nations—that's what I had in mind for you."* I am blessed that I had a praying man in my life. I am blessed that I have a God who always has my best interest at heart. After my engagement, my focus was on planning a wedding, but that wasn't the only thing that God had in store for me.

As we discussed the type of wedding we wanted, we both committed to spending more time on the preparation of our lives together than on the actual wedding. I wanted to do everything differently than the first time I walked down the aisle. Our first step was to schedule some time with the minister of the Apostolic Church that was now becoming Renson's church. For practical purposes, we had to consider the kids' chaotic track-and-field schedule and our availability. I knew that I wanted something small and intimate and only with the people who meant something to us. Ladies, for those who have had a wedding, you know how we get when it comes to planning a wedding. While I was busy thinking about wedding plans—what kind of dress I wanted, how I wanted my body to look, the type of food I wanted to serve, how I would incorporate my boys into my service—the Lord had other plans. His plans involved my soul and my relationship with Him.

My on-and-off relationship with God was something I wrestled with for a long time. There were times I was closest to Him and other times when I was mad at Him. This parent/child relationship that I had with my God was a personal one. I am blessed that He never gave up on me, even when I was rebellious, living my life the way I wanted to and not the way I knew He wanted me to. He never abandoned me. It became customary for all of us to attend church together, and there was nothing special about this Sunday as I prepared to go to church. That's what I thought. But I was so wrong! This particular Sunday was one that I will never forget because the Lord decided to lean in heavily on my heart.

After the minister finished preaching his message, he extended an invitation to come down to the altar for anyone in the sanctuary who hadn't given his/her life to Jesus or someone who knows the Lord but wasn't living a life that was pleasing to him. I didn't want to go down to the altar. The Lord was talking to me, tears began streaming down my face, but I remained in that seat. There was wrestling going on internally. I began thinking I didn't want people to look at me funny if I went down to the altar; I was sure that I looked crazy with makeup running down my face, not to mention how huge my eyes get when I cry. All these thoughts were racing in my head. Instead of rebelling, like I'm known to do in the past, with His help, I got up out of that seat and walked down to the altar to re-dedicate my life to God. When the Lord is ready for you, He is ready—you can run but you certainly can't hide. On that Sunday morning, the Lord was ready for me, and I was ready to turn my life completely over to Him.

January 13, 2019

It's good for us to go to church as a family; Mommy, Renson, Sebastien, Emilien and me. Today, the message was powerful. As I sat in my seat, I was compelled to go to the altar, but I was wrestling with the decision and had made the decision not to. After I made the decision, Mama Persha came beside me to urge me to go down to the altar. This had to be absolutely the work of God because there is no way Ms. Persha could know what I'm thinking. At the altar, Stephanie prayed with me, and I felt the presence of the Lord. Maybe the Lord is giving me the rebirth that I need.

For so many years I've put it as my resolution to get a better relationship with God. This seems to be the right time as things are falling nicely into place. I know this will not be an easy journey as Satan raises his ugly head, but with Jesus by my side, I will be okay.

As I stood at the altar with tears streaming down my face, I felt totally at peace. My makeup was running, my eyes were swollen, but I didn't care. I walked back from the altar a different person. I was at peace, and there was a burning desire in my heart to figure out where the Lord needed me to be. When service was over, my boys kept inquiring what was wrong. They were surprised because they were not accustomed to seeing me crying. I didn't have the words to explain what was happening to me. I wasn't sure what all this meant, but I was on the path that I needed to be on. I walked away with a promise that someone from the church would do a series of Bible study with me to help me understand what the walk with Jesus means for my life. I'm glad that I had Renson and Mom by my side to help me along this journey.

Several months before this, Renson had re-dedicated his life to God and his faith, and now it was my turn. I found myself opening my Bible on other days besides Sundays. I had several one-on-one Bible study sessions where I was getting many of my questions answered. I had numerous questions about the Apostolic faith and some practical questions on dress, demeanor, and what it meant as a woman of faith in the church. *Why can't I cut my hair? Where in the Bible does it say that? How about the long skirts, do I have to wear them? Can my skirts and dress be fashion-forward? How about jewelry, where does the church stand on that?* I found myself digging in the Bible and re-reading the scriptures that were pointed out to me to help answer my questions. When I had questions, Renson kept reminding me that the Holy Spirit would be my guide. Living your life for Christ is not always an easy road. I found that the minute I committed my life to God was when all the problems started exponentially coming my way. I found myself praying and trusting God to guide me. Most days I found myself starting my day by reading my Bible and praying. When I didn't find time to devote to the Lord, I had no covering when the devil attacked.

Palm Sunday 2019 has a special meaning for me. That was the day I turned over my life to the Lord. This was unlike when I was nine years old. This time, I knew exactly what I was getting into. I knew exactly that this was the only way for me to live my purpose-driven life, the one the Lord ordained for me. As Psalms 63:1 states, "Oh God, thou art my God; early will I seek thee: my soul thirtieth for thee, my flesh longest for thee in a dry and thirsty land, where no water is." I took these words with me as I embraced what God has for my life.

April 14, 2019

Today is Palm Sunday and a very special day for me. Jesus is not done with me yet. It was a beautiful service. Surrounded by my family Sebastien, Emilien, Renson and Mommy, I got baptized in Jesus name. This is a rebirth for me. I laid all my sins down when I went under the water, and I came up renewed. I thank God for His grace and favor. Not only did I get baptized, but I also received the Holy Ghost and began speaking in tongues. This was a beautiful moment for me and my Lord. I have a special glow surrounding me. Nothing is by accident, and I'm so grateful that I gave my life to the Lord. I look forward to what the Lord will do in the lives of not just Renson and me but also our children. If someone told me years ago that I would be baptized in an Apostolic Church, I would tell them that they're lying. God is an amazing God. He knows what we need even before we ask.

Sidoney Samuels-Buckridge **231**

Sometimes we run, but we can never hide from God. What I am most grateful for was that my God never gave up on me. Even though I was not deserving, He had mercy on me and welcomed me with an open heart. My Lord Jesus has always had mercy on me from when I was in my mom's womb until I made my way into the world. Sometimes when I think about His grace, my early beginnings flash before my eyes. In 1974, in a third-world country like Jamaica, not many two-pound babies were surviving, but I did because the Lord had a plan for my life. I went through all my challenges in my first marriage because God had a plan for my life. I endured the struggles with Crohn's disease because God had a plan, and He wanted me to use my struggles as a testament to his love and grace. It's only God who can forgive.

Everyone knows that planning a wedding comes with drama. I am so blessed that this time around I was a different person. The Lord was working on me, so when the drama came my way, I had tools in my arsenal to deal with the challenges. I was determined to ensure that I had the wedding that Renson and I wanted, and that was all that mattered. Our minister counseled us on putting God—no one and nothing else— in the center of our marriage. I enjoyed discussions around compromise, looking at challenges from a biblical perspective, and the importance of supporting each other, especially in a blended family. Renson and I were spending time thinking about the type of marriage we wanted and what we needed to make that happen. While we were busy focusing on the marriage we wanted, the wedding challenges came our way.

For practical reasons, we needed to get married before the boys' track season started because we would be tied up at track practices and meets every Saturday during the months of May through August. Initially, we wanted to get married in April; however, we couldn't get a Saturday that would work, and we ended up with May 4, 2019, as our wedding date. When we got that date, I stopped in my tracks and my thoughts screamed, "No way!" My first wedding was the exact same date, and I thought this might be a bad omen. As a child of the King, I recognize that the word *omen* is not in our vocabulary. Being saved gave me that tool in my toolbox to recognize this was the devil trying to get into my head. What God has put together is what God has put together, and the same wedding date had no bearings as long as we were following God's guidance.

The next wedding challenge came in the form of family drama and wedding invitations. Since Renson is from Miami, the bulk of our wedding guests were my family and friends. It was important to me to ensure that only those who meant us well were invited to our union. Now, ladies, I can't be the only one who has family members who claim they love you, but you know that is the farthest thing from the truth. After all, just because someone is related to you by blood doesn't mean they have your best interests at heart. When the drama came, I was prayerful, and I remained calm. The Lord was really working on me. Even I was surprised by my reactions. I acknowledged God and was not leaning on my own understanding. In the past, I relied on myself, and that's what got me in trouble. The difference this time was that I leaned on the Lord to help me with the challenges.

Just because I'm a Christian doesn't mean that my life is perfect. In fact, the minute I began walking with the Lord, the tests were intensified. I'm a firm believer that if you don't have a test, then you won't have a testimony. There were many tests as we prepared to walk down the aisle. Renson and I focused not on the challenges but on the blessings that were bestowed on us. We had so much to be grateful for: We had each other, we had our faith, and we had the support of our families and close friends.

On May 4, 2019, in front of God and 40 of our family and close friends, at the age of 45; I received my second chance at love. I married my best friend and the man whom God deemed to be right for me. Most importantly, I was at a place in my life when I could give freely of myself. I could trust again, and I was allowing God to lead me and guide my path. I was leaning on Him and not on my own will. I had a beautiful wedding because months were spent preparing for our marriage, and our wedding day was a continuation of that journey. My babies, who looked like grown men, were participating in the day too. I was blessed to have my boys, Sebastien and Emilien, walk me down the aisle, and that meant so much to me. I had my two besties by my side, and that meant the world to me. Ladies, sometimes only a girlfriend can prop you up when you are down. I know that Shika and Jackie saw me at my lowest moments, but they never judged. They served as listening ears, offering advice and always being there for me. Having them stand beside me and serving as my bridesmaids was incredibly special. Some ladies have sisters whom they are close to and others have "sister friends." One of the significances of my wedding day was an acknowledgment that I can't plan every single aspect of my life. If I had, I wouldn't have had this opportunity. Everything began to fall in place when I let go and let God.

May 4, 2019

It's my wedding day! I'm up at 5 a.m. of course. Had my devotion and just spending some quiet time by myself before this place becomes filled with people and activities. I plan on savoring the moments. My wedding was beautiful!! The makeup artist came to the house and did my face, and it looked beautiful. Sasha was at the house, and I'm so glad I got some photos with her. My chauffeured car came and my two besties and bridesmaids, Shika and Jackie, not only helped me get ready, but they got me in the car and helped me remain calm and focused on what was about to come. The boys walked me down the aisle, and I couldn't stop laughing, smiling, and giggling because I was just so happy. Our pastor performed a beautiful ceremony. Right after the service, we went outside with the wedding party and immediate family to take photos. After that, the wedding party was introduced: Renson and I were introduced as husband and wife and we did our first dance to the song, "A Love Like This." Everything went well. The food was delicious, the toasts by Shika and Dwayne were lovely. I loved the intimacy of our small wedding. Thank you, God, for blessing our union.

Life Lessons From This Chapter:

- Good things come to those who trust the Lord—trust in the Lord and lean not unto thine own understanding.

- Follow the path that God has for your life— let go and let God.

- Having a relationship with God is not just about going to church—daily praying and reading His word is key.

- Focus on the marriage and the life you want together—not just the wedding.

Chapter 8

LIVING MY BEST LIFE

"I like livin' this kinda life. I'm livin' a blessed
life. I can speak to mountains, they will be
moved. I can speak to dreams, they will come
true. I can tell my troubles to get away. God
gave me the power to make my day."

—*Livin*—song by the Clark Sisters

I am living my best life. You know why? Because God is the author and finisher of my faith. I know that God will help me accomplish my goals now that I've completely committed myself to him. "In all thy ways acknowledge him, and he shall direct thy paths." (Proverbs 3:6) He is leading me every step of the way, and for the first time in my life, I know that I am living the life the Lord ordained for me. I now have a personal relationship with God, and it has made all the difference in the world. Troubles and trials will come my way, but I am no longer fighting my battles alone. I now have the prescription for my success. My career is no longer in my boss' hands; it's in God's hands. My finance is no longer in whatever raise or bonus I do or don't get; it's in God's hands. My family relationship and the rearing of my children are no longer in my own hands; they are in God's hands. Challenges will come my way, but I don't need to worry because God's got this. I just need to live my life by faith and trust God.

There are people who choose to stop living because bad things happen to them. Thankfully, I'm not one of those people. As is evident in this memoir, I've had my share of hardships, but I'm a fighter, and I refuse to just sit back and accept things or to allow my past to dictate my future. Is this the way I imagined my life would be at this point in time? The answer is no, but the life I now have is one that is better than anything I could have imagined. There have been many scars from the experience with my ex-husband. In the past, it was difficult for me to forgive people who hurt me. I have come a long way, and while God is still working on me, I now find that I can let go of hurts, disappointments, and sadness. I have fully embraced my faith and am looking forward to this new life that I have in Christ.

They say that when good things happen, bad things are right around the corner. I was a newlywed and a new convert. As a "baby in Christ," this early walk with Him was not a piece of cake. After my two life-changing events (baptism and marriage), everywhere I turned there were challenges. The Lord's word is a reminder to me that my walk wouldn't be a bed of roses. John 16:32 says, "These things I have spoken to you, that in me ye might have peace. In the world ye shall have tribulations: but be of good cheer; I have overcome the world." The devil was not letting up, but the difference now was that I was not leaning on my own understanding. I had the Lord Jesus guiding me, and I had a husband who was a prayer warrior, helping me bring all my burdens to the Lord's feet. I was comforted by Romans 8:37, "Nay, in all these things we are more than conquerors through him that loved us."

One month after we exchanged our vows, my husband was in a car accident. You see, the God that I serve is a protector and a miracle worker. After dropping our son off at school, he was returning home when an older driver ran into the passenger side of my husband's car. Here is how God works: If that accident had occurred five minutes earlier, our son would have been in the car, and he would have been hurt. The Toyota Camry Renson was driving was totaled, but he walked away from the accident with not even a scratch on him. God was, indeed, in control. We had a testimony of God's grace. The devil was not done with us yet. Two weeks after this incident, the devil tried to get a hold of my youngest son. He was at a track meet and ventured off into a wooded area with his friend. They came to a body of water and tried to cross it, and my son almost got swept away in a sinkhole. Some people call it luck, but I know that luck had nothing to do with it. The Lord Jesus had His hands on my child.

God knows that I wouldn't be able to handle it if something bad were to happen to Renson or Emilien. I got down on my knees and thanked the Lord for His mercies towards me and my family and for keeping my two men safe. When you serve the mighty God that I serve, you don't have to live your life in fear; you just have to trust Him. The challenges and attacks seem to come in threes—first my husband, then my son, and I was not immune because the devil lashed out a personal attack on me as well.

As I grew in my personal relationship with God, I was learning how to deal with the attacks of the devil. Interestingly, the devil doesn't always come with something major to attack Christians. Sometimes, it's not even external forces that the devil uses; oftentimes, he attacks us with doubts. He will lead us to believe that we are not saved because of all the wrong or sinful things we have done in your life. At times, I find the devil challenging me as to whether or not I'm saved. He will bring up something that I have done in the past that was not pleasing to God to lead me to believe that I'm not saved, that I'm not a Christian, and that God has not forgiven me. I found myself agonizing over these thoughts on numerous occasions.

Ladies, I'm going to keep it real with you—sin is sin. At times we try to convince ourselves that some sins are bigger than others, so the little ones don't matter. They do matter. Admittedly, in the past, I didn't always live the life that I knew God wanted me to live, but once I went under that water on April 14, 2019, all my sins were washed away, no matter what the devil wanted me to believe. Yes, I disliked my ex-husband, and initially when I left him, I had malice in my heart. That was a sin. But guess what? That has now been forgiven. Yes, I had sex with someone I wasn't married to, and fornication is a sin, but that too has been forgiven. My relationship with the Lord was getting stronger, so the devil was becoming relentless too. One of his attacks was to work on my mind to cause me to think that my transgressions were so big that they are unforgivable. I am happy that I serve a very forgiving God, a God who is merciful. No matter what the devil threw my way, I was ready because I was no longer walking alone.

During the second half of 2019, I was under immense work stress that manifested itself in a way that was unfamiliar to me. I was accustomed to stress triggering off my Crohn's disease and the abdominal pains that accompany those flareups. This time was different. This series of medical challenges started with a pain in my neck that would not go away. I tried everything. I went to the doctor who informed me that it was muscular. I went to a chiropractor, but I found no relief. After dealing with the neck pain, three weeks later, I started experiencing back spasms. The doctor again confirmed that these were muscular pains that I was experiencing. I wasn't exercising, so I wondered why I was experiencing muscular pains. It got so bad that I ended up in urgent care and given medication to help with the spasms. I never stopped praying because I knew that my God was still in the healing business, and that was exactly what He did. I went to Jamaica for vacation with the pills the doctor prescribed.

I was on the land of my birth, and I did not want to spend my two-week vacation doubled over in pain. I began praying to God to heal me. I started taking daily walks, where I was getting fresh air and observing the beauty of the Caribbean Sea. An amazing thing happened. After a few days in Jamaica, the pain was gone, and I stopped taking the medication. This is how my God works. The devil will not have dominion over me because I know I serve an amazing God. My body's reaction to the stress I was under really scared me. I didn't know that stress could manifest itself in that manner. Crohn's disease I'm awfully familiar with, but all these other symptoms caught me off guard. I'm glad that my homeland is always a place of contentment for me. Perhaps it was the beautiful sunshine, the white sandy beaches, and the beauty all around Jamaica that can bring on these feelings.

I know that I'm a scratched record—for those who are old enough to know what this cliché means—repeating the same things over and over again. But I can't stress enough that God doesn't make mistakes and that His timing is always right. He knew that I needed a partner to help me navigate the challenges that were coming my way, He knew the boys needed a good father figure in their lives, and most importantly, He knew that I needed to get back to a place I once was with Him. As a single mom, I did what I needed to do. I regularly operated on little sleep as I juggled my career and parenting. Once I got a partner sharing the parenting role, I was amazed at how much "me time" I now had. After I got a husband who believes in sharing the load, I now had time to do things for myself. Every woman needs that—whether it's getting your nails done, going to a coffee shop, or just lounging around with a good book. I've come to cherish these "personal times" because someone else was taking the boys to their activities.

I told myself that I was fine being by myself for the rest of my life. I was WRONG! Having the right partnership is great and can be such an asset in a woman's life. Notice, I used the word right. If it's not the right person who makes you feel loved, cherished, and whole, then it's better to be by yourself. This is even more true if the relationship is toxic. What I cherish the most is having someone whom I can always lean on for support, encouragement, and advice. I had to learn to let go and let this man love me and do things for me. Being a single mom for so long, I was used to taking care of everything myself. My life changed, and the family dynamics changed as well, and I had to learn how to accept that. The boys developed their own relationship with my husband, and I had to step back sometimes when they wanted to go to Renson to help them deal with their issues. Change takes time, and the blending of a family is a major change. The boys adapted more quickly than I thought they would. They were watching Renson and me. They were noticing how we negotiated things, how we showed affection, and how we interacted with each other. I always wanted my boys to witness what it looks like when a man and a woman were in a healthy relationship, and for the first time, they did.

During our premarital counseling, the best advice that we received was to put God in the center of our marriage. That's exactly what we try to do on a daily basis. Are we always successful? No. But I've learned that it's easier being married to a man who has a strong faith. Praying together, fasting, and having devotions are all par for the course, and that makes a world of a difference. Following the scriptures has guided us when there are challenges.

Ephesians 4:26 "Be ye angry, and sin not; let not the sun go down upon your wrath" is something we live by. If I need a prayer partner, or if I need him to pray on my behalf, he's there. He knows the right words of encouragement. We share the same faith, so we can uplift each other. What has also occurred is how the boys have begun to embrace our faith. The fights to dress properly and wake up for church diminished until it was no longer an issue. God blessed me until "my cup runneth over." He provided more than I've ever asked.

May 4, 2020

Today is my one-year wedding anniversary! One year just flew by. I have so much to be thankful for. God has continued to bless me and my family. Even as I write this, I am pinching myself because I never saw this life for myself. I'm so glad that God's plan is always so much greater than my own. This is certainly not how Renson and I planned to spend our anniversary due to the COVID-19 pandemic, but what these unprecedented times have taught me is to live in the here and now and to focus on what is important. What is important is that my husband and I lived to see our one-year anniversary and we are happy and in love with each other. I took today off from work, and Renson and I looked through our wedding album and reminisced about our special day. My husband did not disappoint me. We might not be able to go out, but he brought fine dining to me. We got dressed up, and he served me lobster, salmon, and shrimp pasta. Some of the things that have been memorable this year are how Renson embraced my boys, stepping in as the father they need. How he loves me unconditionally, and how he is so giving. Thank you, Lord, for this milestone.

The year 2020 will be forever etched in our minds due to the global COVID-19 pandemic. When the history books are written, I will be able to say, I remember what it was like to live through one of the most historic health crises that took millions of lives from this earth. I was so fortunate that I have a strong faith to help me during those critical times. When people were searching for something or someone to make sense of all that was happening around them, I was blessed to have my family and faith to keep me through a very unprecedented time in the United States and in the world for that matter. As the death toll of fellow Americans began to climb into the hundreds of thousands, there were many stresses and much fear: fear of the unknown, fear of a virus that did not have a cure, and fear of economic downturn.

As a child of God, I chose trust over fear. The Lord said in Isaiah 41:10, "Fear thou not; for I am with thee: be not dismayed; for I am thy God. I will strengthen thee; yea, I will help thee; yea, I will uphold thee with the right hand of my righteousness." I did not need to be fearful because I knew in my heart that my Heavenly Father had it all under control. I had someone to hold on to—Jesus! I put my trust in Him. Of course, watching the death toll rise, hearing from friends who lost loved ones, and witnessing the horror that this disease had on the world affected me because I'm human. What I made sure of was not to live my life in fear because I trust that God would have His way, not only in my life but in all of the earth. That realization brought me peace. A powerful verse, Isiah 26:3-4, helped me through the difficult times. "Thou wilt keep him in perfect peace, whose mind is stayed on thee: because he trusteth in thee. Trust ye the LORD for ever: for in the LORD JEHOVAH is everlasting strength. Our lives were interrupted, and we had to get accustomed to a new normal.

March 27, 2020

The world like we knew it, no longer exists. A global pandemic called Coronavirus or COVID-19 has altered the way we live our lives. It started in China in late December and cases started appearing in the U.S. in early January. This is a highly contagious virus. It's killing people around the world in the thousands. For the last two weeks, all of us have been home. I've been working remotely, while Renson, of course, can't work because he's in the service industry and all restaurants, bars, gyms, and non-essential businesses are closed. We are not permitted to have gatherings of more than ten people and we all have to practice social distancing which is to stay six feet away from others when outside. For the most part, we are home around just our family. School has shut down for the past two weeks and on Monday, March 30th, they will move to online learning for all students in Montgomery County Public Schools. We will all have to wait and see how this will work out. We currently know that the plan is to have the kids out of school for another month until April 24th. Personally, I believe that the date will move and most likely the kids will not go back to school for the rest of the school year, like Virginia schools. This virus has been around for a few weeks and as of today, there are 82,300 cases of infection and 1,100 deaths in the United States. We can choose fear, or we can choose God. We are choosing God and this time has renewed and strengthened our faith. Since all Churches are closed, we have been having services online on Sundays and Wednesdays. God is sending us a sign, and we need to give heed to Him. I pray daily for my two boys' salvation, that the Lord will touch their lives and they will give their lives to Him. Jesus is the only way, the truth, and the light. Will there be challenges because of the virus? Absolutely! Many have lost their jobs and livelihood and the economy is in turmoil. Despite all that, God is able to move mountains, so this too shall pass with His divine intervention. I pray for God's strength to keep me and my family.

While many people were focused on the negative impact of the COVID-19 virus, I decided to focus on the positive side of all this. As a family, we strengthened our faith. Pre-COVID-19, it was typical for us to attend Sunday morning services as a family, but it was difficult for us to get to prayer meetings during the week. Being home and getting the service online, we attended both services weekly as a family. In addition, I got the boys to attend the weekly youth service. A nice side effect of the pandemic was that we were doing more things together as a family.

We live such busy lives that we have no time to sit back and enjoy each other's company. With both boys in competitive track and field, our lives are a juggling act, with getting to practices and track meets on top of everything else. Not having track and with everything being shut down, we had nothing but time. We started getting closer as a family, eating our homemade meals together, worshipping together, and spending quality time with each other. These were activities that we never had time to do, based on hectic work and school schedules and everything in between. The virus slowed the world down, and we decided to take advantage of this great side effect.

As the weeks of quarantine turned into months of stay-at-home, ordered by the Governor of Maryland, I found myself appreciating the simplest of things. I once took a lot for granted. Taking a walk in my neighborhood, going to the grocery store and finding the things I need for my family, and talking on the telephone with loved ones far away became things that I did regularly during the lockdown. My husband and I spent a lot of quality time together talking, making plans, and assuring each other that we would get through this stronger than when we entered it. I began appreciating all the time I had to connect. As an introvert, I am not necessarily known for my sociability, but I found myself gravitating and working hard to be more social with my family. I found myself having more time to listen to the boys as they shared their concerns about our new "normal." At the dinner table, while discussing issues we heard on the news, it was always interesting to hear the perspective of teenagers. They are known to offer unique points of view that differ from adults.

What's next? For me, living my best life means that I will continue to set goals for myself. I will continue to strive in my personal and my professional life. Personally, I'm on a journey, and I want to become the woman God wants me to be. I know He has an enduring purpose for my life. I will let Him lead and I will listen and follow. I am looking forward to my contribution to His Kingdom, whatever that will be and look like. As a mother and wife, I hope to continue to grow in these two important roles. Motherhood comes with no manual, so we all have to figure it out. It even looks different, depending on the needs of your child. I have two very different boys whose requirements from me are not the same. As my young men enter into adulthood, I am looking forward to learning how I can help them become the men I hope they will be. I'm looking forward to my role as more of a listening ear, sounding board, and counselor to them. I have this second chance at love, and as a wife, I hope to continue to grow in that role as well. Marriage is a partnership, and what you put in is what you get out. Marriage requires work, and I am going to roll up my sleeves and partner with my husband to make the marriage one that we both want. I am looking forward to navigating the various seasons that we will experience in our marriage. Most importantly, I am looking forward to growing old with this man whom God has chosen for me.

Professionally, I still have much more growing to do in my career. I believe learning is life-long and particularly important. I have to keep learning and to continue to push the boundaries so that I'm allowed to develop and grow. Corporate America is still trying to figure out what to do with someone like me. As a woman of color, I will continue to brace myself in handling challenges in the workplace. I'm not alone because many women of color all over this country face these challenges daily. I'm passionate about diversity and inclusion and will continue to raise my voice on the topic and do what I can to move the needle in a positive direction. I will continue to mentor, guide, and listen.

Throughout this book, I shared many lessons that I learned along this journey of life. I want to leave you with the two that resonate the most with me:

1. "Don't be defined by your circumstances—fight for what you want."

2. "The Lord is a way maker and a miracle worker—we must have faith in Him."

Society says that the family I was born in, the environment I grew up in, and the color of my skin is a recipe for me to be a statistic—born of a teenage mother living in the ghettos of Jamaica. I defied those statistics, and I charted a different path for myself. From an early age, I was determined to fight for the life I wanted and to not be defined by my socioeconomic background. Ladies, you can do the same thing. Don't let anyone tell you "You can't be this!" or "You can't be that!" I believe we all have the ability to strive for what we want if we are willing to put in the sweat equity. I would be lying if I tell you that it will always be easy. What I can tell you, however, is that you will feel joy when you defy the odds and make the impossible...possible.

I am a walking miracle! I can make this statement because I know that without my faith in Jesus Christ, I would not be the woman I am today. I can testify that the Lord is a way maker and a miracle worker because without Him, the stories I shared in this memoir would have different endings. Having a personal relationship with the Lord serves as my moral compass because He never steers me in the wrong direction. I've often ventured off on my own, but I'm so glad that He never gave up on me and that I found my way back to Him and am now living my best life. My purpose is to be driven by God's plan for my life and to live authentically, both personally and professionally. I will continue to use my gifts, talents, and abilities to help propel others to greatness. By writing this book, I hope I have helped someone on their life's journey.

There are no limits because I won't let boundaries stop me! I will continue to channel the drive and passion of the bright-eyed 16-year-old who set foot on American soil almost thirty years ago. This immigrant will continue to strive and live her American dream.

Life Lessons From This Chapter:

- Being a Christian doesn't mean that you won't have challenges.

- Putting God in the center is the recipe for a good marriage.

- Working on a blended family takes time— change is hard; patience is the key.

ACKNOWLEDGMENTS

First and foremost, I want to thank my Heavenly Father for all the blessings that He has bestowed on me. I am grateful that He has given me the ability to take on this venture. He has given me the gift of turning words into impactful narratives, and most importantly, he has given me the drive to turn my setbacks, pain, and triumphs into something that can help others. Without the Lord by my side every step of the way, this would not be possible. I've always wanted to write a book, but I could never find the right time to devote to it. God's timing is always the right time!

I would not have been successful without the love, help, and support of my village. During the most difficult time of COVID-19 with all of its uncertainties, I embarked on this journey and my family was my loudest cheerleaders. I want to thank my husband, Renson, for his love and belief in me that I could bring my vision to life. He was there to comfort me when the tears started flowing as I reread and attempted to deal with some of the most difficult times in my past. He patiently listened, even though I have repeatedly told him the stories numerous times. He became my sounding board. I know it hadn't been easy for him to watch me go through this, but his comfort and love gave me the strength to push forward.

I'm blessed to have two special ladies in my life who nurtured and shaped me into the woman I am today: my mom, Pearl; and Godmom, Kathryn, who has been more of a mom to me.

251

My story is greatly influenced by my mom, Pearl, and the sacrifices she made to help me every step of the way. She was there for many parts of my journey, and as the book began to take form, I'm grateful that I had her help. She occasionally reminded me of key parts of the story that I forgot. I want to thank her also for allowing me to share information about her life and journey. For that, I have to say a big thank you. It's not easy to open up your life to the world, but she knows how important this is to me, so she did not hesitate. Not only is Mom one of my biggest advocates, but her entrepreneurial mindset kicked in when I started the writing process. She began devising her plans of how she can market and get sales for my book. I was pleasantly surprised to hear her friends say they couldn't wait to read my book. Mom was already securing sales before the book was even written. That's how much she believed in me!

From an early age, Kathryn encouraged me to write my thoughts down. In fact, she bought me my first journal. I thank her for the inspiration. I know she probably thought I was crazy when I told her I was going to write the book during the pandemic, with everyone at home, while I juggled a heavy workload and a new work environment, but she never uttered those words. She encouraged me and repeated her mantra for me: "You always land on your feet." Hearing her say that motivated me because she has seen me at my best and my worst. As one of my first readers, her feedback and comments were what I needed to continue to push forward. Kathryn, thanks for your support and for always believing in me.

Those of you who have children or are around them know that teenagers can be finicky and brutally honest, with no regard to how their words impact others. When I started writing, I was at a track meet for my younger son Emilien, and I was typing away on my iPad. Unbeknownst to me, my oldest son Sebastien was sitting behind me and reading what I was typing. He commented that my story was boring...ouch! Coming from a 15-year-old, that is no surprise. As my project progressed and I began sharing tidbits with him, I could see the pride on his face that I was pushing hard to become a published author. Of course, he would never say that because that's not "cool" at this age. Emilien was fine with my writing, but his only concern was whether or not he would get a free copy of the book because he can't afford to use his allowance money to purchase my book. Despite their bantering, I have to thank my boys because they gave me the inspiration to fight for myself and to work hard to accomplish my goals. They were depending on me, and I could not let them down. When I was at my lowest, all I needed to do was look in the faces of these precious children that God gave me and I knew everything would be all right somehow.

My village would not be complete without my besties Jackie and Shika. Jackie, you have been beside me every step of the way during this writing project. You've spent countless hours on the phone with me as the project began to take form. You listened, guided, and challenged me, which made my product better. I value your candor, and your input is so greatly appreciated. You were the first person who set eyes on this book because I trusted your opinion and I knew that you would =spending hours reading and editing my early drafts and then getting on the phone with me so that we could discuss ways in which I could improve my story. This process had a nice side effect; I believe it strengthened our friendship, and we were able to share things with each other on a deeper level. Thank you for all your help and guidance. Shika, thank you for pushing me to realize a dream that I've had for so long: to be an author. When it got difficult and I felt like giving up, you wouldn't let me. Thanks for serving as a sounding board as I wrestled with what I could or should share. Thanks for keeping me honest so that I could be my authentic self. Friendships are so important, and I am blessed to have these two women in my life who were part of my journey and who continue to support me in all my endeavors.

When I started this project, I knew nothing about the publishing industry. I quickly learned that writing was only half of the equation and that I had a lot to learn, especially if I didn't want to fall prey to what happens to a lot of first-time authors. Lucky for me, I have people in my network who are knowledgeable and are able to guide me through the process. I have several people that I want to thank, including my friend and colleague Sara, who not only chose my wedding photographer but was also instrumental in designing my book cover. Sara also coached me through the ins and out of the publishing industry and encouraged me to do a photoshoot so that she could get the right photo to design the cover. The shoot was daunting, and I went kicking and screaming. But in the moment and afterward, it was an amazing experience. I truly appreciate Sara for pushing me out of my comfort zone, helping me hire a wonderful photographer Vijah, and for being a friend who did not tell me what I wanted to hear, but what I needed to hear, to bring my vision to light.

Editing is a key part of this writing journey. This is my story, so I am very close to it, which means I would have blind spots. Thanks to my early editors, Jackie and Sabreena, for your help and advice. Thank you, Dr. Lonnell Johnson (content and copyeditor), for taking my manuscript and giving it the thorough editing it needed to bring my vision to fruition. I appreciate the homework and reading assignments you gave me. They helped to improve my craft. Thank you for pushing me to reconsider my initial title and also for encouraging me to share some of the scriptures and quotes that mean so much to me. Thank you, Eliza Enriquez (proofreader) for your keen eye that added the finishing touches. To my amazing production team: Sara Lamont (graphic designer), Carlene Vitale (book designer), and Vijah Britto (photographer).

There are so many people to thank, and I cannot name everyone individually, but you know who you are. Thanks to those who have inspired me, my early mentors, Andy and David in Jamaica, and my later mentors who have helped shape me. Life is a journey and finding one's purpose is not easy, but I'm glad I did. My purpose is to be driven by God's plan for my life and to live authentically, both personally and professionally. I will use my gifts, talents, and abilities to help propel others to greatness. With God's help and the support of my family and friends, I will continue to live my life according to His plan.

ABOUT THE AUTHOR

Sidoney Samuels-Buckridge is a native of Kingston, Jamaica, who emigrated to the United States as a teenager. She is an award-winning communications professional with more than 20 years' experience in public relations, journalism, corporate affairs, and executive engagement in various industries. She has a bachelor's degree in communications from Elizabethtown College and a master's degree in mass communications from the University of South Carolina. Sidoney lives in Maryland with her husband, two sons, and her mother. She enjoys playing Scrabble, working out, and self-care. Sidoney is an avid reader and has written several published articles. This is her first book.

Website: sidoneysamuels.com

Facebook.com/Sidoneysamuelsbuckridge

Instagram.com/sidoneysamuelsbuckridge

Twitter.com/SidoneySamuelsB

Made in USA - Kendallville, IN
1224262_9781736138809
01.13.2021 0954